# The Fabric of
# Consciousness

# The Fabric of Consciousness

Sergio Santos
Matteo Chiesa
Maritsa Kissamitaki

# THE FABRIC OF CONSCIOUSNESS

iUniverse books may be ordered through booksellers or by contacting:

iUniverse
1663 Liberty Drive
Bloomington, IN 47403
www.iuniverse.com
1-800-Authors (1-800-288-4677)

ISBN: 978-1-5320-5675-8 (sc)
ISBN: 978-1-5320-5676-5 (e)

Print information available on the last page.

iUniverse rev. date: 09/18/2018

# Contents

# Dedication

This book is dedicated to all the people that spent many hours discussing the topic of the mind with the authors and to those that with their actions alone have made us think.

# Preface to the first edition

This short book is an invitation to thinking around the meaning of the terms consciousness, reality, logics, truth and human. It is also a book that centers on the mind, not in the sense that we want to scientifically describe the brain, its parts and its functions. We describe the mind in that with the mind we can attend to what the world, ourselves and others have to say. The mind might further allow us to position ourselves in the world and stand or confront it with a view. We use the mind to read signs and orient our thinking toward that which calls us for attention and holds us. In this way the world orients us as we orient it back as if in a back and forth sway. Is the mind a tool for logics, coherence and the grasping of emotions? This book comes at a time when predictive AI and definitions of intelligence are expected to overwhelm humans with logics and evidence that anchor to a reality constructed with strong and reasonable arguments. The object of reality in humans is thus understood as a debate toward a target: a search in the name of the curious word "truth" that is otherwise exploited through the other curious words termed "logics", "reality" and "evidence" to act as a weapon to defeat, overrule and protect our stance with conviction. As metaphysics, religion and ethics totter and collapse in front of our eyes, we find ourselves with a task at hand and the will to materialize it. In this way, we experience the words "truth" and "logics" dissolving as smoke in every turn, but also embrace them as familiar confronting weapons that act for or against us.

In these chapters we describe the condition of humans by circumventing and questioning metaphysical words such as truth and logics in favor of a descriptive language. We invoke the human in as far as humans find themselves in the condition of confronting, tarrying or giving up on their world. As humans, we hold onto who we are by leaning toward that which holds us. We hold back onto that which holds us and term reality this reciprocal holding by claiming with it our position in the world and toward it. The object of our reality is otherwise and always facing the possibility to collapse and totter as we face a sway or sudden shock. As the directiveness of our everyday lives are exposed to a world that totters in its foundations, we are pressured to stand firm and grounded in a position to confront it. We might otherwise attend to the sway and face a position of discomfort and disconcertment that menaces to collapse our world. In this way the sway involved in the listening to the call for attention stands against the answer that is delivered at hand. The idea that swaying is to be avoided delivers with it an unread sign that signals a direction toward the call that guides our theme. The world offers us all, from science, to sports, arts and motivational books, as supporting guides to direct and orient us. Our own orientation otherwise menaces to emerge at any time as a floating boat that, as if astray, drifts toward no land. The interaction with the new era of argumentative weaponry will challenge our sway and attempt to provide us with a direction in a way that new technologies are threatening already. In such era of technology and connectedness we envisage the coming of a human-object that disregards the possibility of swaying and is already and at all time engaged and with a sentence and a task at hand. With a sentence and a task at hand, humans appear as if unconscious and unaware of the direction they assume as they pressure toward their path. In the meantime, and in the middle of such turmoil of words, dissolving truths and ambiguity, new technologies such as AI and the laws that come with them are emerging.

The first two chapters act as an introduction to 1) the current state of metaphysics and 2) the foundation and take-off of fields of science such as artificial intelligence (AI) and the coming of governmental laws in these emerging fields. Otherwise the first two chapters might be skipped, and the reader might directly jump onto the description of the mind. The first two chapters are the most challenging conceptually but do not contain our description of the mind fully. They are otherwise general in that they point to what comes next by directing our theme. When words or sentences appear in between quotation marks we are telling the reader that the meaning of the words is to be considered carefully, that standard meaning might not apply or that we are using a metaphysical term to be explored in the whole of the work. We note that some quotes of Nietzsche and others are repeated a few times in the book to familiarize the reader with the phenomena that we explore. The quotes are many times written after a paragraph and left for an open interpretation or to be interpreted by the reader directly from the text in the book.

There is further no hiding of the fact that this book is deeply based on the methodology of questioning of the foundations of metaphysics and the position of science by Martin Heidegger.

We emphasize once more that our criticism in favor of avoiding the abuse of terms is otherwise not intended in a negative way, as if implying that terms can always be employed clearly. Our criticism is always directed toward avoiding metaphysical terms to misguide the questioning and thus preventing possible phenomena to emerge naturally. This point is also key in the decision to employ the methodology of Heidegger and in quoting pre-Socratic thinkers. Still, this does not clarify our quoting what could be regarded as just hanging sentences from thinkers rather than structured and precise modern definitions or modern scientific findings and methods. In this respect, we ask the reader to formulate the following question: If words are vague or not clear, or even if we are missing something regarding the emerging phenomena of the mind, how could we know? Before moving to our argument, we recommend the reader to ponder this question.

As we question, we "say", and as we "say" we are somehow already directing our questioning into a direction of our own. That today we "are" open minded enough to explore the whole of what "is" cannot be just "said". Through our questioning we are already involved in the metaphysics and ontology of the humans that we are today. If we are to say what the mind is and to claim that we see it for what it "is", we are to use language to orient our questioning while also mistrusting it. By reading the ancient writings, the metaphysics and historic metaphysical load of terms might clarify if we can tell what the mind "is". If the phenomenology method, in as far as we describe the phenomena and stay out from abusing modern terms or modern mechanisms of biology or other, is to grant us the access to see what "is" with diluted modern metaphysics, we will be in a position to interpret the ancient Greeks in a more original way. This seeing in a more original way should result in unveiling what our metaphysics veil. Whether the ancient Greeks saw "the truth" or not is also not our major concern since such discussion would directly send us back to the path of modern metaphysics. In this sense we advise the reader to think about what we say and question rather than to continuously look for "truth" in the sense of what the modern word truth is to say. If anything about humans has remained, we could find it in our everyday language as we speak to ourselves and to others. In that everyday speaking we shall find a connection with ancient Greece that we might not find in academic or formal work. Our language is then to provide us with direction in our search. It is then not coincidental that we quote many times Nietzsche here, as he dealt with the ancient Greeks very intensely throughout his career and he spoke of what "is" invoking what and who we "truly" are. In summary, our work is meant to be an invitation to thinking and exploring that which the mind "is". If the topic is raveled by empty or ambiguous words, questioning such words might allow us unravelling it. It might be that what we humans are is at stake today more than ever as advancing technologies might simply tell us what it is that we "are". As we explore what the mind is, we are exploring who we are in a time where what we are might come to us delivered as a violent placing.

We further warn the reader that our work is not meant to be "logical" in the sense of standard textbooks on logics. Our work is meant to make us think, so it is an invitation to thinking. With this we clarify that standard logics, such as propositional, mathematical or other logic, are not taken here as the instrument of thought or thinking itself. Our work is then to bring phenomena to the front, so we can acknowledge it as phenomena of the mind. The analysis is also preliminary in that we are challenging current views but do not pretend to have the final say on the topic. Finally, the intention is to write two more follow ups. One on the foundations of truth, reality and logics and another on the concept of the human-object. We expect these three books to act as a foundation to a theory of mind expressed in the language of mathematics and exploiting current scientific findings from neurology to psychology to implement it. With this we clarify and acknowledge that our analysis here is not complete.

This book is largely based on ideas in three works by Martin Heidegger:

Heidegger, M., *What Is Called Thinking?* 1976: Harper Perennial.
Heidegger, M., *Introduction to Metaphysics*. 2014: Yale University Press.
Heidegger, M., *Being and Time*. 2010: SUNY Press

# Introduction

## The mind

The philosopher of mind John Searle was quoted to have said:

> *"There is nothing that we are more used to than consciousness but at the same time there is nothing that we understand the least - John Searle"*

If we pay close attention to the above line, we might hear that even when we are used to a term like "consciousness" we might fail to understand it. That this term and references to its theme continuously appear in our everyday lives however implies that we understand it somehow. The term and the phenomena that we refer to is in this way "familiar" to us. A question already comes to mind: if a term appears to be familiar, how can it also appear to be "ununderstandable" or at least "inarticulable"[1]? That the foundations of, and reference to, phenomena by a "word" appear as ungraspable when one sets to clarify what one means, no matter how familiar the word is, is also "familiar" to us. Let that be that we just got mysteriously acquainted with a word, because what a word meant to mean drifted into oblivion or simply because a word sometimes does not actually mean anything, that is, it is empty or used as a general undetermined term. The line seems to say that the difficulty to understand "consciousness" will persist irrespectively of whether one gets into the etymology of the word in the hope to get "acquainted" with it in as far as its historical origin, evolving meaning or usage. This might be because as one is already acquainted and even most used to using words, any more familiarity with them might not get us any closer to their meaning. Yet, the terms being "used to" and being "familiar with" imply a form of "understanding" that also strikes us with "familiarly" as fundamental and basic. As we say we are "familiar" with something we seem to say that we "know" its theme and "understand it". As some form of circularity manifests in our questioning, we meet other seemingly "ambiguous" terms. In this case for example, it is not the term consciousness alone that lacks clarity in the sentence of Searle. The term "understanding" is also at stake. In any case, what does it mean that we "truly" know or "understand"? That we "truly" understand something implies that we are very familiar with it in a sense that we are "close" to it in a way that all that is essential about it "comes together as a whole" in our thoughts as we think it. Such "sayings" regarding "understanding" also sound familiar, even if we consider them somehow deficient. Subtle phenomena strike more than anything else when we think about what we have said already. Already in our initial attempt at questioning the word "consciousness", we seem to have relegated the study of "consciousness" to the study of "understanding". This is surprisingly striking and thought-provoking. That words are familiar but still ungraspable many times drives us to other words that are equally familiar and ungraspable as in a circle that seems to be playing games. Such playing games and circularity in saying also appears as "familiar". Heidegger once said:

> "If we may talk here of playing games at all, it is not we
> who play with words; rather, the essence of language plays
> with us ... - Heidegger."

What appears as circular in "language" and "understanding" has been discussed since ancient times. When speaking of the human condition and "understanding truth" Parmenides wrote[2] about 2500 years ago:

> *"Deaf and dumb and blind and stupid, unreasoning cattle -*
> *Herds that are wont to think Being and Non-Being one and*
> *the self-same[3], Yet not one and the same; and that all things*
> *move in a circle. – Parmenides."*

Heraclitus[4] also said at around the same time:

> *"Gathered in itself, the same is the beginning and the end in*
> *the circumference of the circle. – Heraclitus."*

We now want to state at once that even when our thinking and speaking appears as circular, or as if playing games, this does not impede us getting "familiar" with words, or with the phenomena that they refer to, in order to gain "clarity". On the other hand, we are not to discuss words in as far as "words" here. Rather, emerging circularity might lead us into a direction where formulating questions gets us ever "more familiar" with the phenomena of the mind and "consciousness". What we seek is the emergent "positive" phenomena of the mind. Whether such phenomena appear from enquiring words or other, we are to stay close to "phenomena" so to not lose site of it. What has emerged so far can be put in the form of questions already: what is this familiarity with "things" and what things "are"? Is this familiarity something relevant or merely something to be dismissed as "obvious", already "understood" or even "empty"? What is this "ignoring" or "obviating" the words that appear together with the phenomena that most stubbornly emerge as most familiar to us in our everyday lives?

The essence of language and speaking is coming to meet us even through advancing technologies. Emerging fields such as AI come up with virtual assistants, chat-bots or other to "speak" and "listen" to us. Experts in all fields come together from computer sciences to linguistics, semantics, psychology and machine learning to create these "talking" machines that also "listen". While still relatively rudimentary, these technologies are rapidly advancing in a direction toward a target so what they almost do now they will excel at soon. These entities have memory and access to databases of knowledge that help them "know" everything at once. They have the answer ready at hand. These AI entities have the target to "understand" humans while getting "familiar" and "used to" us as we, in turn, familiarize ourselves with them. These AI entities might also "understand" our lives in as far as they can advise us and assist us in our everyday lives in order to do or know that which "is needed". Yet, as we interact with current technologies, the very nature of our everyday lives appears as "ungraspable" to them. As they "know" our lives, our lives appear "alien" to them in that they do not "know" what our lives are. In this way, what we are "used to" the most, even if we seem to "understand" the least, appears as that which strikes us the most as lacking in these AI entities. That is, in as far as there seems to be a "separation" or a "gap" between that which we "know as familiar" and that which we just "know", these AI entities miss the most where something strikes us as most "familiar" and "ungraspable".

The ancient Greek philosopher Heraclitus wrote:

> *"For they turn their backs on that with which they traffic the most, λόγος, and what they run into every day appears alien to them. – Heraclitus."*

We provide an alternative translation:

> *"The λόγος: though humans associate with it most closely, yet they are separated from it, and those things which they encounter daily seem to them strange. – Heraclitus."*

What λόγος is meant to invoke in the above sentence belongs to a whole exploration that is our theme. Suffice it to say for now that it has to do with "saying", "hearing" and "understanding". In any case, the separation between that which we know and that which strikes us as "most familiar" does not appear as a smooth separation either, but as a clear cut that presents itself as an "abyss" of ambiguity and circular unknows. As soon as we try to define it, we have a "gut feeling" that there is something missing that leaves us as uneasy as with the tip of an iceberg that we just barely make out. Yet, as we just barely make out what is missing, we also have this "gut feeling" that we already "know" what we mean so well, that we will always be able to tell if there is something missing. This separation or gap that has emerged in the introduction so far motivates our next formal question.

Is there a separation between that which we "know" and that which we know as most "familiar"? We certainly might know how to use a smartphone, yet philosophers of mind like Searle claim that we don't understand what consciousness is even though we deal with it continuously. Could it be that this familiar and obvious phenomenon of "not understanding" but "knowing" is hiding what we "are" in a fundamental way? It might be that the more we obviate "the familiar", the more we drift away from it. This is even when every day we "know" more about ourselves through science and technology. That machine learning, big data, neurology and other technical fields know more about us every day through algorithms and advanced instrumentation might then leave us at a loss regarding the "what" and the "is" of humans. The separation might even exacerbate the more we direct our advances toward that which we know as that which we are "most familiar with" buries under terms. That that which appears as "most familiar" might not come to the surface when we ask ourselves the question of the "what" and the "is" of what the human mind "is" motivates our exploration in this work. That we rapidly ask for definitions of things to put what things "are" into "words", so we can "know" them, is also to be explored as phenomena.

Heidegger used the term "proximally" accompanied with the words "for the most part" in a way that he would write "proximally and for the most part". We are to use these words to pay close attention to the phenomena of the mind and the phenomena of "obviation". To use these words however we need to somehow already understand them. So, what does it mean that phenomena appear "proximally and for the most part"? That something appears proximally and for the most part implies that something strikes us in a sense that it is "close" or "familiar" to us as it comes as a thought, mention or question. It also means that something is familiar in a way that it already appears as such even when we first mention it or think about it. For example, when we question "consciousness" it strikes us as "familiar" even in the first attempt at questioning or clarifying what it means to us. Such familiar phenomena also come for the most part in the sense that we seem to already know what the matter of the phenomena is in all its ambits. This is even if such knowing is not particularly clear in that we do not manage to articulate what we "know" of it clearly. The implication is that whatever we miss in the phenomena as we explore it, will strike us at once as "there being something missing". Missing not in that a small part is missing, but rather, in that some "very relevant" part is missing without which the phenomena seems to not have been fundamentally grasped at all. We will also notice that there is something missing irrespectively of how clearly or well explored all other parts are. "Consciousness" is in this way familiar but "ungraspable" when we try to articulate what we mean with this term. Yet, proximally and for the most part we "understand" consciousness. The difficulty of articulating what we mean worsens the more we use words such as "truth", "reality" and "logics" to clarify the meaning of terms. The more general the terms, the more we appear to leave "something missing". Furthermore, such "something missing" in any exploration that "misses something" strikes us in a way that terms seem to involve some sort of "wholeness". That is, terms and phenomena do not want to be analyzed in "parts" that can be held up or put together into one later. The phenomena that emerge in this way in any exploration of the mind appear in this sense as "equiprimordial". That is, we cannot "grasp" what we mean by just invoking parts that miss others, but we cannot find "a fundamental part" that involves it all either.

The physicist and philosopher of mind David Bohm wrote[5]:

> *"What is required is not an explanation ... Rather, what is needed is an act of understanding; ... incorporating (all) ... in a single movement in which analysis into separate parts has no meaning. - David Bohm."*

David referred in the above sentence to a seeming separateness of "thought" and what is being "thought about", i.e. the real, presumably as the "object of thought" that might initially come as a "thing" and as if separate from "thought".

In his speech on truth[6] Parmenides wrote:

> *"Consider how far things have a strong presence to mind: in fact (the mind) will not separate the being which holds narrow to the being either when it appears fully scattered everywhere in the cosmos or when it appears joined together. – Parmenides."*

That ancient Greeks were already concerned with explicating the "coming together" in the mind of what "is" might as well anticipate the full separation of mind and physical brain by Rene Descartes about 400 years ago. Such separation might strike us as academic. On the other hand, this tendency to separate what "is" in the saying of what "is" as opposed to what we claim "truly is", sometimes relegated to what "refers" to what partly "is", "opinions", "appearances" or "points of view", also emerges as everyday phenomena in that it appears as "familiar" to us. That there is a tendency to separate what otherwise "comes together" in this type of duality, such as the thought-thing duality, was emphasized by Heidegger in his reading of the pre-Socratics. To gain access to what it would be to understand what "is" in a less "mature" metaphysical age, Heidegger interpreted "saying" and "speaking" as what ancient Greeks referred to as λόγος. This is the λόγος of Heraclitus above.

> *"What is said in λόγος as what comes together, implies that what can be understood is understood by what is already conforming – Heidegger."*

In the above sentence, the meaning of "what can be understood" refers to the term "conforming". We are dealing again with a "word" and an exchange of words. In this sense, unless we already "know" and "understand" what this "already conforming" means, we have gained no further insight into λόγος nor saying. The question then emerges: what does "already conforming" mean? This "already conforming" will be explored in the following chapters but a preliminary interpretation will be given in the next pages. We will also reread the sentence above after a small detour. In any case, duality presents itself so strongly that David Bohm also wrote:

> *"Can there be no further insight into the relationship of thing and thought? We suggest that such further insight is in fact possible but that requires looking at the question in a different way. To show the "orientation" involved in this way, we may consider ... an analogy ... - David Bohm."*

David Bohm is in fact "explaining thought" as he finds himself on his way "toward thinking" thought. In his thinking about thought Bohm invites us to follow him toward a thought by "reorienting" ourselves toward that which comes in his "saying". If we pay close attention, we might notice that Bohm invokes a "reorientation" in order to "see". We might see this reorienting as a leaning toward a call for "seeing" what remains otherwise and for now "concealed" to us. In summary, the sentences above claim that provided we do not "reorient" ourselves we will not "see" the further insight. This would be the case no matter how firmly and positively we analyzed the arguments given from our current "orientation". That is, no matter how "logical" we were to sound. An implication would be that deploying "logics", machine learning, predictors or exploiting big data might not lead us to "seeing" any better unless we "followed his advice or suggestion" to first reorient. We would not "see" any better by exploiting standard logics from textbooks nor "logical reasoning" described in metaphysical methodologies such as Hegel's dialectics either.

In the fragment already cited above Parmenides also wrote:

> *"If much I talk, you listen and accept my speech, which only ways of inquiry are thinkable: the first: that (being) is and that it is not not-being, is the way of Persuasion (in fact it accompanies the Truth) – Parmenides."*

If we do not take the words "you listen and accept" as an instruction to "obey" but rather as an invitation to "not lose track" of what the speaker has to say, that is, as suggesting the listener to be "guided" by the speech, we might "not lose sight" of what Parmenides is saying. If we want to "listen" to his saying, we must "lean toward" his invitation or call. After he invites us to "listen", he talks about what "is", in the sense that it "is", but also in the sense that what "is" is never what "it is not". While such saying might sound odd, it is not uncommon in our everyday lives to say things like: "What you said is not what I meant (said)." or "You are misleading what I said into something I did not mean (say)." or "You put it in other words but got exactly what I said.". These sayings come as "familiar" to all that speak but we are not to take the implications for granted. In the quote above, Bohm invokes a reorientation, that is, that we see things in another way and in a way that he has otherwise seen already. Parmenides uses the word "persuasion" (some translating this term as conviction or belief) in his fragment on truth while "Bohm" uses the somehow similar saying "We suggest that ..." to "persuade" us when he refers to seeing the "truth" of the matter at hand that he "sees already".

That persuasion and suggestion are common in our everyday language is noted as one lives, reads signs and is "guided" by people in all sorts of environments and through all sorts of daily issues and activities. We many times start sentences with "I believe that ..." or "I suggest to you that ...". We also ask for guidance: "Could you show me the way to ..." or "How is this meant to work according to you?". In all such sayings there is directionality in as far as a direction is given as we "say". There is also a tendency to position oneself toward what is said. Before one can "see" things and "think" in a way and "toward" a thought, one must position oneself in a way that "things" can be "seen" for what they "are". Bohm is "asking" us to already take a position or view before we can see what is to follow and explain to us what he "sees". Put in the form of a question: is Bohm saying in the quote above that he wants to "guide" us in order for us to "see"? In other words, Bohm is asking us to "position ourselves" and "orient" ourselves toward his "sayings" before we attempt to "understand" them. For us to "see", Bohm is asking us, similarly to Parmenides in his speech, to "already conform". This takes us again to Heidegger:

> "What is said in λόγος as what comes together, implies that what can be understood is understood by what is already conforming – Heidegger."

In his writings on thinking Heidegger also wrote:

> "Only when we are so inclined toward what in itself is to be thought about, only then are we capable to think - Heidegger"

The leaning toward what is to be thought about is also a theme of this book and it is explored in terms of what this leaning might mean. We further explore how this "leaning" or orienting oneself toward a thought relates to being "conscious". Before we do so however we quote a well-known sentence of Heidegger regarding thinking and then interpret it.

> "Everything thought-provoking gives us to think ... as far as it already is intrinsically what must be thought about... Most thought-provoking is that we are still not thinking – Heidegger."

From the above lines the most "striking" might be the term thought-provoking. People currently use the term thought-provoking everywhere in a way that it might catch our attention. Other words such as "truth", "reality", "logics" and "thinking" might be used in a similar way. The use of words to catch our attention is not what we are terming here "leaning toward" a call or "listening". That is, one rapidly loses site of the sentence if one looks at what is striking rather than to that which calls for thought. This happens in our everyday lives continuously as one says to another: "That is not what I meant.", "You changed the meaning of what I said.", "You literally quote me but out of context." or "You don't even listen.". The last way of telling someone that they missed "what we said" is particularly intriguing since it implies that while one might "hear" and get all the words said, one might still miss "listening" and therefore understand nothing. This missing does not refer here to how well one knows the language of communication or technical methods. That is, that one improves a given microphone or algorithm to understand "sound waves" and turn them to "words" is not what we refer to in here as to "better hear" or even "understand at all". We don't refer to "understanding" in that one might get all the "words" and "logically unfold their meaning" in a way that "they make sense" either. This is not the case even when one exploits the best neurology techniques or linguistics methods. With such procedures, one might rather fully misdirect the meaning of what was said so to get in fact farther away from what was said as one unfolds logics more strongly. Other times we say, "I hear you." or "I'm listening." meaning "We understood.". The "listening" is closer to the "I'm leaning toward you". We might further add to the latter: "But I don't hear you." as if we are "missing" what is said even when "Listening.". This mysterious "hearing" but not "listening" or "hearing" in the "saying" is also to be explored here. As if invoking such "hearing" but not "listening" Heraclitus[7] wrote:

> *"Those who hear without the power to understand are like deaf people; Present, they are absent. – Heraclitus."*

What we pay most attention to according to Heraclitus has nothing to do with "ears" or "eyes":

> *"Eyes and ears are bad witnesses for people, since their souls lack understanding. – Heraclitus."*

Parmenides also wrote regarding the "misguiding" of the "eyes" and "ears":

> *"But you remove your thought (mind) from this way of inquiry nor long habit push you along this way, to direct the eye that does not look and the resounding ear. – Parmenides."*

So, what is Heidegger telling us regarding the most thought-provoking? He is telling us that we are still not thinking. Yet, that we are still not thinking might not be noticed as striking in the sentence as we lose sight of what the saying says. As the sentence guides us, we guide it, and while the guiding occurs directionally, its own original direction might be "missed". In this way, the more the term "thought-provoking" is merely employed, the more the essence of its saying dissolves into nothingness. Words turn to smoke if we lose site and reference regarding the "toward" and the "toward where" as they were meant to originally guide. As we say, provided we speak for something rather than chatter, we guide and measure. As we "say" we provide "direction" and "guidance". The ancient Greek Protagoras has a very popular saying that we might read and interpret from our discussion so far:

> *"The human is the measure of all things. – Protagoras."*

When our "hearing" and "saying" loses direction, words might "acquire" a direction of their own. Media, news, rumors, gossip and repeating a sentence are examples of ambits where words might "lose their original direction" while acquiring their own. In these, the dissolving of original directions and the emergence of other is particularly stubborn. Words on the other hand, do not always have the character of referring directly to what "is", even originally, and might be deliberately fraudulent in what we commonly term "lie" or "deceiving word". This way of lying is considered here but it is not the only nor even the main way of "deceiving". On the other hand, we acknowledge that it might play a big role in the difficulty to understand in that "as one listens" one might "always end up deceived". Nietzsche said of lying[8]:

> *"The liar is a person who uses the valid designations, the words, in order to make something which is unreal appear*

*to be real… they hate (presumably people) … not deception itself, but rather the unpleasant, hated consequences of certain sorts of deception. -Nietzsche."*

That is, the word might "deceive" in as far as it is originally conceived to lead us astray. We emphasize however that it is not this "deceiving" only that we are dealing with in this book. But rather, we deal also with the "not hearing", even as "one listens" and with the "seeing or hearing other."

Nietzsche commonly spoke of language in parables and as to the losing of a reference through language:

*"Life is a well of joy; but where the rabble drinks too, all wells are poisoned … when they called their dirty dreams "pleasure", they poisoned the language too – Nietzsche."*

Nietzsche found the idea of "mere words" most amusing and wrote[9]:

*"Most books are born from the smoke and vapor of the brain: and to vapor and smoke may they well return. For having no fire within themselves, they shall be visited with fire – Nietzsche."*

Nietzsche might have been talking about books that say "nothing" even though they contain words in them. This "saying nothing" is again intriguing and it is to be explored here in connection to "ambiguity". We also claim that one might "exploit" words that were just "heard". As soon as the word is heard the word appears to be "owned". The word "acquires" a direction of its own. This word that was just said and acquires a direction of its own is ubiquitously appearing everywhere from social media and news to politics, ethics and the issues in our everyday lives. Once one says, the "word" is what "is" in the "direction" that it takes. This is what we mean when we refer to an inherent directionality of the "word" and the direction that a word might acquire. The directionality of the word also appears as a "telling" of the "who" of the person. That is, the person that "says" exposes the "who" of who they "are" to others and to themselves.

The word that is said might also appear as the "word" being said but not "its saying". As in the thought-provoking expression, the word might appear as what "is" where the "saying" is just missed or ignored. The exploiting of words that emerge as smoke in all ambits of life is not considered by us as positive or negative phenomena in general, at least preliminarily in these first works. We would be violating the requirement to closely attend to the phenomena that emerge from the workings of the mind if we did so. If any, it is the emergence of the phenomenon that appears as the "mere use of words" in all ambits of life, including the writing of books, as what "is", that we consider a "positive phenomenon" that emerges in the theme of the mind. The emergence of such phenomena indicates a form of "directionality" of the word that "guides" the mind as the mind reciprocally guides the word. This is irrespective of whether words or "deceptions" are uncomprehended, a priory perceived as negative or futile in the phenomena of the mind. Using words that appear as just words and using words that acquire their own direction is then constitutive of the mind. The use of words in this way however appears as suspicious if one labels them "thoughts" or, in any case, "related to thinking". That such use of words is otherwise common in our everyday lives also hints at the possibility that "thinking" might not be the only or even the main way in which the mind operates. At least in the standard meaning we give to the cogito of Descartes where humans are those who "think" so they "are". Let alone that thinking is to do mainly with following logics at least in the standard sense that we might understand such "following logics". What we refer to, proximally and for the most part, when we have the term "cogito" in mind, is a way of thinking related to "pointing toward" that which is otherwise still "unknown" in that we are "to think it". Heidegger expressed the theme of thinking in three sentences:

> "When humans are drawing into what withdraws, they point
> to what withdraws. We point to what is still uncomprehended.
> We are an uninterpreted sign – Heidegger."

These three sentences will also be explored in the next chapters in that with the mind we point and in that this "pointing" is there to be explored. That we are an uninterpreted sign in that we are on our way toward a thought is taken as an emergent "positive" phenomenon of the mind, even if such "toward" presents itself only as a possibility. That the "mind" is inclined by necessity toward a "toward" as an "still uninterpreted sign", that is, that directionality in the gathering of thoughts guides the mind toward a "a toward", was also tacitly implied by Bohm:

> *"… this step (the initial step in which thought properly begins)*
> *arises very early as a necessary stage in the attempt of thought*
> *to bring sanity and order to its "dance" – David Bohm."*

In summary, we are to explore the mind and its phenomena to gain clarity regarding what the mind is. We are to initiate our exploration by securing a way to explore such phenomena. The terms "mind", "consciousness", "reality", "logics", "truth", "thinking" and similar appear "proximally and for the most part" as coming together with the phenomena of the mind. These are possible initial candidates to explore in as far as we could list them, describe them and define them to then connect them to the phenomena and workings of the mind. That these words appear to "come together" however does not mean that they are "equiprimordial" in terms of the phenomena. Let alone that we can just add together definitions of these terms, as if glued together, so the mind and consciousness is then fully grasped theoretically to then be modelled. As noted in the introduction, these words might appear just to misguide and "deceive" us as they are loaded with metaphysical meaning that many times seems incomprehensible. We are then to pay close attention to the phenomena that "proximally and for the most part" emerge in our exploration of the mind instead. Phenomena will emerge as "familiar" and "close to us" but otherwise "ambiguously" as if obviated in relation to the "whole of the phenomena of the mind". The emergence of this phenomena will also be brought to the surface as something that "emerges" in such exploration. That is, the emergence of phenomena itself is to be considered in as far as its emergence and not only as what emerges from it. This emergence, no matter how obvious might appear to us, will be considered "positively". We use the term positive in that, provided phenomena emerge, there is "something" emerging and there is also "emergence" and the structure of emergence.

We claim at once that phenomena have already come to the surface in this introduction. This happened as soon as we mentioned the term "consciousness". A first "positive" phenomenon to emerge relating to the mind itself is the "being used to words" and the "being used to using words" that are very "familiar" but otherwise and somehow "not understood". Words and "saying" also emerge with an inherent directionality in that they point and guide into a given direction. Emergent phenomena will be considered, at least preliminarily in our theme, as constitutive of the structure of the mind as "pre-ontological" structure, yet not "ontical". We will not get to the meaning of "pre-ontology" and "ontology" here however[10]. We will leave these terms unattended instead to already provide a clear direction to this book: a search of "positive" phenomena that emerge as structure of the mind as the "what" and the "is" of the mind. We will further take such positive phenomena as a possibility. Possibility in that phenomena might not always emerge. In fact, it might not emerge at all. In its inherent condition of "possibility" however, "positive" phenomena still dictate the "is" of the mind in that without considering it, we would be "missing" what we mean with the term "mind" as a whole. With the questions that opened in this introduction regarding the mind, understanding, saying and language we start the exploration of the mind.

## The structure of the question

The theme here is the "mind" as the phenomena of the mind appear to humans. Such phenomena however are to be accessed in one way or another. As if daring, we take as our guiding direction what we somehow already know of the mind as phenomena in our everyday lives. We dare because even if "words" and "phenomena" are known already to refer to this or that word or phenomena, these are not to be taken for granted. Rather, the phenomenon is to be always kept close to the explication and to us. This method is subtle in that we take the words and phenomena that we "know" in our everyday lives to "guide" us. These words and phenomena are otherwise to be always mistrusted in that words are already guiding the phenomena to an interpretation that might already be metaphysically oriented. Words and metaphysics are always persistent and stubborn. These might appear in all ambits as if attempting to dissolve any clarity or as if continuously redirecting any field or "ungrounding it" toward emptiness or a "mere word". This "ungrounding" appears as if rejecting all attempts to "truly" ground. For example, the physicist Bell wrote in his book "The speakable and unspeakable in quantum mechanics":

> "Here I would entertain the hypothesis that experimenters have free will. But according to CHS (Clauser, Horne and Shimony) it would not be permissible for me to justify the assumption of free variables "by relying on a metaphysics which has not been proved and which may well be false. "Disgrace indeed, to be caught in a metaphysical position – Bell."

The notion of a "last step" required to ground a theory appearing as if "metaphysically ungraspable", "ungrounded" or as if reduced to a "word" is recurrent and stubborn and can be found in fundamental articles on the "reality" of quantum mechanics even today. Talking to phys.org[11] R. Renner[12] said in 2012:

> "Our result is based on the assumption that an experimenter can, in principle, 'freely' choose which measurements he would like to carry out ...Hence, if one is ready to accept this assumption, our answer can be considered final. However, it is certainly legitimate to question this 'free choice' assumption (as well as the way 'free choice' is defined). – Renner"

Taking such risk into account, we are then gaining access to the theme of the "mind" from the "positive" phenomena that emerge in our everyday lives. Such phenomena shall provide the orientation and direction of our description as we approach the phenomena from that which we somehow already know. As we are already "acquainted" with the phenomena we are also risking to "obviate" its emergence by pushing it to the side to focus on that which is not obvious. In this way, it is the "obviousness" of what we already know that will appear most difficult to capture if such phenomena indeed appear in a similar way to that which we term "consciousness". That we know then, does not mean that we know a word, function or the mechanisms to which the phenomena relegate. That is,

we are not interested in words that academically, formally or informally mean this or that phenomena as obviated with a word placed in place of the phenomena. We are not interested in "intellectualism" either as if, provided we find a relatively nice definition that is not insufferable in terms of internal contradictions, we can move forward neglecting "obvious" everyday phenomena of the mind that appear to be "not important". The phenomena that appear as closely familiar to us already is therefore not to be relegated to other fields of knowledge that have words or known functions that mean this or that if these are similarly "distracting". The main target is not to borrow terms from specialized fields as in deferring or relegating to other. Here, we are to pay attention to the phenomena and question it as its structure emerges. That is, the structure of the phenomena is to emerge and be faced. At this point we can state what our question is.

Our question relates to the "mind" as to the "what" of the question. That is, the "what" in terms of what is enquired is "the mind". The enquiry relates to "what the mind is" and how "consciousness emerges in humans" provided that consciousness emerges at all. "What the mind is" is therefore "what is asked" to the "what". The formal question is: what is the mind? "What is to be found" relates to the phenomena that emerge in as far as it emerges as the "structure of the mind" and as "already familiar". The emerging of the phenomena is also the "what" of "what is to be found". The enquirer is always us, as we already find ourselves in the middle of "dealing with the mind" and the "phenomena of the mind" that appears as "already familiar". In this structure that emerges as the answer to the "what is", and in reference to the workings of the mind, we shall attempt to find the answer to the "is" of the mind, provided it emerges at all.

Our task is then to explore emergent "positive phenomena" regarding the mind as we ask the question "what is the mind?". The descriptive analysis of the mind here is meant to attack any metaphysical bias that does not look at the phenomena straight in the face. Saying that the mind is so and so and that technological advances should be directed in this or that way because of an otherwise ambiguously grounded principle is taken as a fundamental "because I say so" in our exploration. In other words, we do not accept sayings such as we are to think "positively" because it is

"healthy" and brings "happiness" on average. We do not accept it because a "direction", that is, a "toward", is not what we are seeking here. What "drives" the mind, for example "will to power", "will to truth" or "truth", is not an answer to the question of the phenomena of the mind either. That a "because I say so" of metaphysical terms is explicated in terms of mechanisms or functions, no matter how sophisticated these might be, from fields of science or other, does not imply that the explication is other than a "storyline" if the matter of the "because I say so" is simply relegated to mechanisms or other violently placed words. In other words, that "happiness" is based on "peace of mind" and that "peace of mind" is based on the concentration of dopamine and serotonin in a specific area of the brain is not providing an answer to the phenomena of the mind. Instead, such method is explicating the mechanistic origins of a term, i.e. happiness, that we might otherwise take as a "direction" or a "toward" based on a "should" in as far as we are told "we should be happy". That there "is no unique should" will not be taken as an answer either. Basing our phenomenology on what could otherwise be understood as metaphysically sacred and primordial foundations was taken as tantamount to ambiguous and floating tautologies for the theme. Not avoiding sacrificing "sacred" terms or philosophical positions while avoiding falling into metaphysical terms, otherwise appearing as distorted tautologies, is thus taken as a fundamental basis in our description here. This leads us to analyze the structure of the mind as phenomena that occurs equiprimordially in the fashion that the methodology of Heidegger analyses the structure of the question of being. Therefore, the emerging phenomena in this book as well as our description should also be taken as preliminary explorations. If the phenomena that emerge is ultimately emerging as "ungrounded", such lack of ground will also be looked at in the face as "positive" emergent phenomena. If we succeed at all, we should demystify the mind and release the interpretation of the phenomena of the mind from the burden of metaphysical words placed as if these were to be found in a position of depth that cannot be found, or otherwise trivialized as a mechanism explicated fundamentally as the "toward" of a "word".

# The Grounding Ground and
# The Ungrounded Ground

## The is, the need and the obviousness of what we are

With the advances of neuroscience, functional brain mapping, sophisticated brain scanning techniques, stimulants, brain regulators in the form of pills, self-help books, meditation techniques, mind theory, AI developers, mind theory, life advice centres or platforms and other, a bridging of the gap between "what one is and needs" to "what one knows of the brain and the biology of who we are" is being established. The claim here is that such bridge risks to appear as the semblance or shadow of a bridge but might nonetheless come forth ungrounded when one looks at it in the face. That such bridge can be built, so to speak, is otherwise not so clear and even less clear how such enterprise will not totter from its foundations by simply overlooking, ignoring or obviating its foundations. Even less clear is the foundation or grounding of the "is" and the "need" of what we are and need, as given by the "direction" of fields that are taken as an obvious field fit for the task at hand. One could even question the directing of society and scientific advances based on a "need" of humans or what a human "is". If anything, that society is and needs what it is claimed it is and needs, presupposes an ontology of what humans are and need and of the "is" and "need" as an unquestionable starting point. That such ontologies are ambiguously articulated, have many interconnected interpretations or many open fronts does not speak in favour of what we say a human "is" or "needs" either. One cannot simply accept that things remain ambiguously expressed just because the matter at hand is complex and then set forth into a rigorously directed path based on such ambiguous placing by invoking "clarity" or "obviousness". These actions are blatantly and fraudulently violating their own claims. Such proceedings are trickery at best while otherwise ubiquitous in all ambits of life including those that supposedly guide us in life and guide society as whole. Complexity or triviality are not here to be exploited to obviate or derive the questions posed in terms of what the mind "is" or consciousness "is meant to mean". Such derivations speak even less clearly of the direction of what "we should do" as a species based on an "is" and a "need" that is placed in front of us as what is primordial because it is said to be so. Trivializing the "obviousness" of exposing the ungrounded bones of a structure of thought claiming that such exposure is only an over complicated explanation of saying things are not clear is not accepted either. That we find things to not be clear and still act would, if any, hint at "positive" emergent phenomena of the mind. That is, it hints at the mind being "directed" by an otherwise unarticulated "obviousness" that we supposedly "see" as clear but do not bother to articulate, neglect or other.

"Obviousness" as a grounding ground is also not accepted here in the sense that such referring to the "obvious" is not taken as a legitimate method to confront the questions that we pose in our theme. This is more so unless one accepts "ambiguity" and "obviousness" as an uprooting ground, that is, uprooting of the "is" and "need" as emergent "positive" phenomena of the mind. This is particularly so when society and people are indeed acting based on strong claims and "clear" positions that dictate a "clear" direction. The direction is "clear" in as far as there is an act orchestrated through a "toward" and an "end" even if the "toward" and the "end" are not clearly stated nor questioned, but violently placed. For example, technology is advancing "toward" automation and autonomous performance. The respective "need" and "toward" is accepted, even if ambiguously or non-unanimously acknowledged when "confronting society" or each other, in that "it is happening" and it is being debated in the "formal institutions" where we "live alongside others"[13]. This "living alongside others" is particularly intriguing in that many times we do not "know" who we "are" with others but there might be an "is" and a "need" that we "share" with others. The "obviousness" of "living alongside others" as necessary and as a "need at hand" is thus worth questioning since it presents itself as particularly "obviated" and "familiar" to the mind. In such circumstances and in questioning our "living alongside others", other "selves" might emerge as our "I". For example, we might encounter our "living without others" or more simply our "being alone with ourselves". We might also encounter our "true deep self" or our "I". That we deal continuously with the "what" and the "who" of who we are, even if we never question it fully, thus presents itself as "familiar" and striking. The "I" and the "self" are now the target of our discussion in that phenomena of the mind are to emerge.

In our everyday lives we find ourselves saying: "There are more important things that we need.", "You don't know me." or "This is who I am for better or worse." In our "living alongside others" we agree and disagree as to what "is" and as to what is "needed". On the other hand, we rarely focus on the questioning of the emergence of the "is" and "need" phenomenologically. For example, the "is" and "need" might emerge even when, as we find ourselves "without others", we don't know "who" we "are" or what we "need". In many cases, in society and in our "living alongside others", "abstract entities"[14] claim to target "equality" and "freedom of speech" while "campaigning against that which is not tolerable" in a way that "what is freedom of speech" and "not tolerable" remains unclear and ultimately unattended. Still such "movements" take place in clear directions even if intractable and ambiguous when considered jointly in our "living alongside others" or when we are alone "without others". Such sayings are claimed to be "clear" and "unambiguous" or one might simply "shrug it off". We might also be for or against them. In our daily lives, even in our "living without others" and in the "proximity" of our "I" we "move on with life" to dinner, family, work or other. In all cases there is a "toward", even if ambiguously articulated or not fully accepted by what we term our "true deep self". Moreover, in our "living alongside others" our "true deep self" dilutes to the "others" in that there is "this which is clearly known" by ourselves or others. As we "live alongside others" we "need" to be "fruitful" and look "toward" that which "ought to be done". That one "needs" to be "fruitful" and "build toward" rather than "dissolve" structures of thought to "advance" society might be clear to us when said in our "living alongside others". Such sayings however are already "directed" and therefore not the theme here in terms of the "positive" phenomena of the mind that emerge as structure. If any, these "sayings" and "toward" are already standing on the "structure of the mind" and therefore do not relate to the question of the structure of the mind but rather directly "exploit" it. In other words, dismissing the questioning of the grounding of the "toward", "need" or "function" by labelling them "meaningless" or "unfruitful" is just another way to put forth a foundation in terms of a "because I say so" in our "living alongside others". When we find ourselves "living alongside others", let that be in formal settings, institutions or with family or friends, our mind "is" directed by "ourselves and others" in our "merging our discussion with others". The saying of these "sayings" and the emergence of the "is", "need" and "toward" as we are with others, is emergent phenomena of the mind that we encounter as familiar. Whether the "is" is "fully known" by us or others is thus not our concern here. Our concern is that as we "live alongside others", an "is" and a "need" might emerge, even if ungrounded, obviated or ambiguous. We might say to others: "I need to get a job.", "I need to go shopping later." or "I should gain/lose weight." In as far as we say, we have "a task at hand" and we appear as "knowing".

In "our living alongside others" we otherwise might say to others that "we see" that something is not clear. Through such sayings we might "laugh together" or "shrug it off together" to then sometimes encounter our "true deep self" questioning the claims accepted by our "I" when we are with "others". There is emerging phenomena in our distance from "living alongside others" or "with others" and our "finding ourselves with our I". That is, as we find "ourselves without the others", in a sense that we are now not "directly discussing or considering the others", we find "ourselves with our I" and maybe "facing" it. In such facing our "I" we might find an "is" and a "need" at hand. This "I" might not "see" the same "direction", "toward", "lack of ambiguity", "need" and "clear end" that our "I" of our "being ourselves alongside others" "sees". We might term such "I" our "true deep self" in that there is a separation or distance between our questioning, or the emergence of an "is" "need", "toward" and "ought to" in our "being ourselves without others" and our "living alongside others" or our "being with others". That is, when we find ourselves "living alongside others" we are "ourselves with others" as opposed to the self that we think we "truly are". In such finding our different "selves" we might appreciate a "distance". Such distance gives rise to metaphysical terms such as "deep self", "spirit" or other. The emerging "positive" phenomena of the mind however is the "distance" or "separation" appearing as we confront phenomena such as "is", "need" and "toward". Whether there is a "true" "true deep self" or not is taken here as a metaphysical discussion that is not considered in terms of its being true in the standard, and sometimes ambiguous, way that we might understand truth. That is, regarding the phenomena of the mind, the different "selves" emerge as a distance between what we "say" or "see" that "is" the "need" and the "toward" at hand. The "is", "need" or other might otherwise appear as ambiguous questioning. Sometimes we find ourselves "stuffed" or "saturated" with "needs" and what "is" or the "toward" of a given "need". In such situations we might wish we could get out of it all. Nevertheless, phenomena still emerge and the "is", "need", "toward" and "in order to" keep coming to face us in our everyday lives when we are with others or ourselves without others. That others "are" something to "us" also implies that we "see" what others "are". What we say others "are" is to us what they "are" as we know of it even when we say we "understand" there might be "more to them". We mention what others are in our everyday lives continuously as we say: "They are very good at repairing the car." or "Don't go there. They are scammers." We now come to what Heidegger said in terms of what we "see" that others "are" in that such "seeing" pertains to the theme of the mind:

> *"In that with which we concern ourselves environmentally the Others are encountered as what they are; they are what they do – Heidegger."*

In our seeing others for what they "are", which is sometimes trivialized or just mentioned with a shrug, sound, body motion or other, we see the "is" of others. In the same way that we "see" and argue the "is", "need", "toward" and "in order to" of others we sometimes say: "I have this guy figured out!", "I know you well" or "I don't understand the actions of these guys.". In as far as we know others we "see" and "feel" the distance between ourselves and others and position ourselves in terms of our "is", "need", "toward" and "in order to". The flow between such mentioning the "is" of us and others generates "understanding" of the "is", "need" and other metaphysical concepts that are considered "knowledge" by some and "deception" by others. Heraclitus wrote:

> *"People would not have known the name of justice if these things (the opposites) were not. – Heraclitus."*

In this way we orient ourselves with an "is" and a "need" that appears, proximally and for the most part, known to us even if we do not articulate it. When our "is" and "need" as seen by others is disputed we might say: "You just don't know.", "You have your opinion and I have mine." or "I can't put it into words but I know." The phenomena of the mind emerge then as "knowing" what we are and what others are in as far as we "continuously deal" with what we are and with what others are. Such continuously dealing with what we and others are however is mostly left unattended when disputed by others or when simply not being able to tell exactly the "is" or what the "need" is. Many times, we push the issue to the side to "deal with our lives" so others might see that we don't deal with who "we are" even though we do that which is seen by others as what "we are." In this type of situation, there is also the expectation of a "true deep self" emerging at any time as others "understand" from what "we do" but we "see" that they just "don't know us". In this way we constantly live in a situation of "clarifying" to ourselves and others who we are in that while it is not expressed clearly, we also never find time to clarify it fully. The feeling is such that we "see" that part of "ourselves has not been expressed fully" but it might soon. We always have "issues" to deal with that are "about to emerge" anytime. Even in the condition of "mental peace" we live exposed to a sudden "emergence" of who we are "truly". Thus, at anytime we might "see" another side of ourselves and others emerging as "deep selves" or "strange selves". In between this turmoil of words telling who we are, what we need and issues that we are about to deal with, we still claim "we know." That this claim is clearly founded is far from unambiguous. The foundation of "who" we are and what our "needs" are seems rather founded on an uprooting of the saying "who" we are. That is, it presents itself as an ungrounded ground that uproots with no supporting ground. We might anytime "experience" such uprooting as a "happening" that might be later "obviated" by our being alone "without others self" or our "being with others self".

## The task at hand as an ungrounded ground that uproots

In our "living our lives" - with our "true deep self" or as we "live alongside others" - we encounter ourselves "concerned" with metaphysics, "serious" things or those things that "ought to be done by us" because "we ought to do them". Many of these "positions" and "stances" thus relegate what seems to be concerning to what "is" concerning encountered as a "task at hand". We "need to deal" with this task at hand with others, with what we term our "deep self" or any other "selves". The "task at hand" might be known to others that we believe "know" the actual "is", "need" and "toward" of the task. Otherwise it might be known to us but not to others what the task at hand "truly is". The task at hand is always considered a serious reason that legitimates to push everything else to the side. When we encounter a task at hand and we are questioned regarding our metaphysical standing we might claim: "Don't you see this is important?" or "This is not the time." Other times we are overwhelmed and can't cope anymore with metaphysics or "reality", so we need to "deal with our needs" or just "relax". Relaxing might imply not thinking of what "is" or the "need" at hand "seriously" but just chatter instead. In our dealing with "the task at hand" we might feel "happy", "fulfilled", "indignant" or other. The task at hand thus provides an "is" and a "need" that we deal with in our everyday lives even if obviated or ignored as an "is" or "need". As we already deal with an "is" and a "need" we might not "have time" to deal with other things. Discussion on "truth", "reality" or the meaning of what truly "is" appears as an inconvenience to be pushed to the side as the "task at hand" comes to the front. Sometimes "the task at hand" is considered the "inconvenience" but it "must" be done.

Relegating the question of a grounding ground to a more serious task at hand however, i.e. directing and guiding our lives or society into a direction that presents itself as legitimate or clear as such, does not indicate that the question for the "foundations" of what directs us is not legitimate. But rather, that the pressuring objects and directions that we put everything else aside for so to deal with something that is otherwise "truly serious, compelling and legitimate" are taken as the "true" emerging "is" and "need" at hand. Again, if any objects appear as the "is" and "need" at hand they must be looked at in the face, so the emerging phenomena of the mind is brought to the surface. In this way, in our "being conscious" we move from the metaphysics that tells us about our "beliefs" to our "everyday reality" that emerges as a pressuring concern. The use of words such as "is", "need", "should", "in order to" and any other terms where metaphysics typically flourishes as if "uprooting", is as unavoidable as is acting as one lives. As in the case of the foundations of the sciences, metaphysics stubbornly forces its appearance no matter how one tries to "flee". The "uprooting" of metaphysics drives us toward an "abyss" of "ambiguous unknowns" and makes its appearance. Metaphysics meets us as if "untried" in every occasion. It is in this sense typical to hear sentences that go: "Sorry but I don't have time for that!", "I need to get on with my everyday stuff!", "Let's not waste our time philosophizing!", "There's no point to go around in circles!", or "That's life! What do you want?". In such cases we are still "directed" by the directionality of what it "is" that we "need" and the "is" of what it "is to be done" as we "face the world". That is, even as we act as if we don't have time for metaphysics, we can't escape them and still conform with an "is" and a "need". In this way, even when trying to avoid facing the foundations of metaphysics, we "find our way". Such phenomena are "emergent" phenomena of the mind and it is the structure of such emergence that is sought and questioned here. The ancient Greek Sophocles[15] wrote:

> *"Into the sounding of the word, as well, and into wind-swift all-understanding he found his way, and into the mettle to rule over cities.*
>
> *Everywhere trying out, underway; untried, with no way out he comes to Nothing. - Sophocles."*

The concept of what we as a species are and the very drive that directs our lives is otherwise dissolving into words that appear, as Nietzsche said, as smoke. Smoke that shakes the foundations that drive our lives as they totter with the pressure of the word appearing as mere opinion but that otherwise acts strongly pushing everything else to the side. Values are similarly claimed to be rooted in the explanatory mechanisms of biology, sociology or anthropology, to name a few, as these happen to be this or that way because of whatever set of events that took place as a happening that follows a path in the way of a storyline. Anthropology, neurology, and physics, for the sake of mentioning a few again, provide the explanatory mechanisms of how life came to be and what dictates what it is and how it has come to be. These floating grounds provide a "need" at hand in the form of a violent placing: there is a "need" because that need "is". Sometimes the mechanisms that these fields discover are said to be fundamental. Other times these are envisaged as functional. Functional in that a part of the brain or other is explored and explained as giving rise to a so-called function that flows like the mechanisms in a clock. In any case, storylines leave us with a placing of "what one is and needs" that is structurally equivalent to a "because I say so". Eventually, we move on to the "toward" of our lives as the "true" phenomena that come to face us emerge as "real" in what is otherwise metaphysically "ambiguously" attended. In this way, we might grow "weary" of life as we attend it by "pushing metaphysics to the side" or we might embrace a "toward" confidently as we long for what seems to be building ahead of us to our "end". Concerning the sciences – and politics, ethics, or other themes involving institutions - we might comply via our "true deep self" that also finds itself dealing with our "living alongside others". In this way, in the institution we might find ourselves "building" that "which metaphysically seems to concern us" as it involves a "toward". As far as we find ourselves in the institution, equivalent to "our living alongside others" but now formally structured, the "toward" "needs to be". We might then confront the "reality" of the life that presents itself in front of us when we are "without others" and maybe with our "true deep self" or simply in a floating and ambiguous "state of mind" that has "lost a self without others". In our daily routine with others however, we more easily encounter an "is", a "need" and a "toward". In this finding others we "pressure ourselves" to articulate an "is" and a "need" with a hope to "agree with others" or to "confront them successfully." For example, most introductions in science start with a "need" and a "toward" that is otherwise "obviated" as "a correct, necessary or obvious toward". In sciences we might claim that our "toward" relates to improving health, roads or safety. Such themes are "agreed to be correct as we deal with others". A "positive" emergent phenomenon of the mind thus appears in our finding and creating our "toward" as we are and deal with others informally but also formally in the institution[16]. The direction relates to these commonly agreed and accepted "toward" and "need". In ethics, philosophy of mind or other, the theme of the mind might be equally unattended as we build a theory of AI or theory of mind in our dealing with life that we push aside to then "deal with life". The "need" and the "is" is protected in the institution, i.e. academia, hospitals, governments or other, by the "being near and working alongside others" in a structure of power as discussed by Foucault[17]. The matter of metaphysics, even if formally explored in the routine of the academic life, the formal laws debated by politicians or the idle talk that occurs in the "living alongside others", remains concerning but alien to that which "is" in life. The metaphysics of the "is" and "need" in the institution is a "formal" seeking for the "is" and "need" that does not necessarily emerge ambiguously as we "live our lives". Through such formal "seeking" one "thinks" about the "is" and the "need". The metaphysics of our everydayness however are to be encountered by our "true deep self" in our everyday lives or by our "living alongside others" outside the institution. This "self" can now have a different or even opposite "is" and "need" that confronts the "is" and "need" of our other selves. We reread here the saying of Heraclitus:

> *"People would not have known the name of justice if these things (the opposites) were not. – Heraclitus."*

On the other hand, it is when and while we live our lives that we "see" our path "toward" that which comes to face us and "concerns" us. The inertia of "facing others in the directed institution" also appears as a guide where an alien life is discussed while we can forget the actuality of our lives by "discussing it with others". We must emphasize that such discussing with others is "thinking" in as far as we understand "thinking" in the sciences or other, no matter how unrelated such thinking might be to our "encountering" the "real phenomena" that we face in what we term "our deeper life" or our "true deep self". That is, the "dealing with others", "living alongside others", the discussing what life "is" and the "needs of life" with others is "emergent" phenomena in that it emerges as "who we are" in terms of the phenomena of the mind. How does such phenomena of the mind relate to the "direction" of society and the "is" and "need" that drives society? Most of the advances of science and "directions" that the sciences might take, in terms of the "toward" and the "end", come in such "living alongside others" and discussing what life "is" and the "what" and "needs" of life with others in such formal contexts. In the formal context we never seem to have "time" to fully clarify anything. Things are left unattended because we could not do more or do other. In the formal context however, after we "say", things are "said" and "understood" for what things "are" until we "find a chance" to "say other". The chance to "say" other is there as a possibility to clarify the misunderstood in what "is" and the "need". The chance is there in our "living alongside others" and the chance thus depends on us but also others. The direction, the "is" and the "need" of the sciences, formal regulations and laws take a definite form because things have been "said" even if they were somehow unattended, ambiguous or misinterpreted according to our "true deep self" or our "being ourselves with others". Even more, in these formal contexts the direction of society and the direction of the advances of the sciences might take place fully even if "our real needs" appear as alien to such "toward" and "end" and even if the "direction of these" appear as "alien" to us in what we "perceive" to be our "true and deep life or self". Such phenomena that occur as we "live alongside others" seems to "hide" who we "are" to others and might even hide it to our "true deep self". This "hiding" also appears as a distance or separation, in terms of what we "believe" that "is" and what we "believe" the need at hand "is", to our different "selves". The "I" that believes the "is", "sees" a distance as a difference between what the beliefs, or actions that conform to an "is" and "need", of a given "I" or "self" are relative to the other "selves". This is even when we just barely notice the distance, or when it appears "ambiguously" to any of our "selves" since we just "feel" it as "real". Such phenomena, including the feeling of hiding as distance, are the "is" of what we "are" to others and what we "are" to "ourselves with others" in terms of "deceiving".

The emerging "is" and "need" at hand that we have discussed so far, in the sense that there are phenomena emerging, are not to be obviated or claimed to be "nothing". Such phenomenon "is" something in as far as it emerges as phenomena of the mind and concerns the human mind and its "directionality". Furthermore, that there is a "distance" between the "beliefs" of the "selves" does not impede to "do our job" by attending "our task at hand". That is, mostly and for the most part, we can do our job even when we "know" of such distances, in a way that it does not appear suspicious to others as we carry on with what others consider our task to be. Thus, in our living our everyday lives, we might cope with such distances either as we confront the distances, laugh them off, ignore them or shrug them off. In this way, we might find philosophy Professors cheating on their wives or sexually assaulting people at work while teaching socially "acceptable" philosophy and ethics or theorizing about "social reality"[18]. We might find NGOs that socially fight for the "poor" and their "rights"[19] or guides and guardians of ethics or religion[20] to emerge as sexual abusers. We might find politicians claiming to believe in justice and supporting a cause in front of some to then actively oppose such cause or any justice in front of others. We might find activists fighting for equality that would otherwise take an opportunity to become rich even if fraudulently. Heidegger himself was caught in the Nazi movement, and even though his philosophy involves ontological clarification, he presumably never clarified the meaning of his involvement. We might also find ourselves claiming that our "true and deep self" does not agree with what we "do" in our everyday lives as we find ourselves "living alongside others". On the other hand, we might say that "truly" we "are not" that which we do when "being ourselves with others". As our different "selves" do things, such "selves" do what they "need" to do even if such "doing" is not accepted by our "other selves", so there is a "discussion" between our "selves". The discussion might end up abruptly, ambiguously or cause us to be indignant or other as we typically move on the "task at hand" of our everyday lives as the task comes. Such contradictions, distances or separations between what we do and "agree/disagree with" regarding either our "true deep self", our "living alongside others self" or our "ambiguous self that has lost itself" is emergent phenomena. Pushing to the side "deep philosophy" and "fundamental explanations" to deal with "real phenomena" that appear as "true real phenomena" in our everyday lives also emerges as fundamental structure of the mind. The separation between that which is what "is" and the need which is a "need" in the "living alongside others" as compared to that of our other "selves" also appears as emergent phenomena of the mind. We can ask the question regarding "advance" once more after this discussion. Put as a formal question: how might science and society advance and in which direction? It is likely that by the "is" and the "need" that emerge in the "living alongside others" that otherwise veils the "is" and the "need" that emerge as our "true and deep self". In between the discussions that take place "amongst" the different "selves", the "is" and "need" at hand might shake and take a different direction. The "true deep self", for example, always appears as a possibility to shake the "is" and the "need" that directs a general and abstract direction in society. What we claim here in terms of the "what" of the "drive" that drives the "is" and "need" also applies to the emergence of new science, politics, technological advances and events in society. That this is the situation now and it was different before however is not what we claim here. Heraclitus already said:

> *"The sleeping are workmen (and fellow-workers) in what happens in the world – Heraclitus."*

The "true and deep self" label is also worth mentioning here. We label one of our "selves" as "true and deep" in relation to that use of words that we tend to use. We do not imply that there is something "deep", or even a "subject" that is us that is "deep", in the sense that it is less or more relevant, honest or correct than the rest. It is also not "deep" in the sense that it is our "true" "I", has more information about "us" or does things that belong to "us" in a more meaningful way. Structurally, to the mind, all selves are "selves" that we call "I". The "selves" are "selves" in that there are phenomena that "distinguishes" them in our talking about our "I". For example, the separation or distance between the "is" and "need". So how is the "deep self" "deep"? The more the separation between "selves" remains protected and distinguishable, the "deeper" we find this "deep self" to be. With the agreements and disagreements between the different "selves" the distance between them varies and changes as the "is" and "need" at hand of each of the selves change relative to the others. We might call this "our" being different in different places. Sometimes the difference shortens in that there seems to us to be agreement between our "selves" and we might say: "I am at peace with myself." In this way, writings, governmental decisions, news agencies, academic journals and other forms of public or personal opinions speak to our "living alongside others" while remain alien to our "true and deep self", whether we articulate it or not, as long as there is a distance. The flow of information between these "selves" is an emergent "positive" phenomenon of the mind. Through such flow we might feel or present ourselves as indignant to our "true deep self", our "living alongside others self" or our otherwise "ambiguous sense of self" and other times "we feel proud of our selves" or "happy with ourselves" to ourselves or others. The feeling indignant, resentful, proud, happy with or other presents itself through the directionality of the mind as a "toward" and an "in order to" of what "ought to be" as measured by the separation between the "selves". This separation sometimes results in agreement and sometimes in disagreement. We might find an agreement to be "logical" or "correct" and claim that this "feeling" that we somehow "feel" "is" correct so it "is" what "ought to be". How are these "selves" and the respective emerging phenomena giving place to an "in order to", a "toward" or other affect a grounding ground or an otherwise lack of grounding? That such "toward" and "in order to" or other present themselves as "correct" in the sense that "they make sense", are "logical" or "we feel make sense" cannot act as a grounding ground. That is, these still present themselves as a "because I say so" no matter how indignant or proud one might feel when one "sees" an event, "acts" or "thinks" in a given way. Such "because I say so" might also be relegated to what "others know" or to what "we know with others" or to what "others think of us or what we say". In summary, all these remain a "because I say so". On the other hand, the more "ambiguous" and entangled with "metaphysics" the "true deep self", the "laughing with others self", the "shrugging it off self" and the "separation or distance between our multiple selves", the more these "sayings" emerge with the semblance of grounding grounds that "seem to make sense", or, more radically, are "true" and "real". They are "ambiguous" and somehow "deep to us" the more they remain "unarticulated". The grounds also emerge as a semblance of grounding grounds when one seems to see something as "very obvious". For example, happiness or peace of mind might emerge as obvious grounding grounds that are agreed upon between our "selves" and with others. No matter how "obvious" such phenomena might sound however, the reduction to the "saying" that we clearly "see" what is obvious in the grounding, results in an uprooting ground. Uprooting in that the grounding ground appears as "groundless" as one explores it. Here, we are not to negate the validity of living according to an "uprooting" ground such as happiness or other. Such validity might be in accord with its grounding and therefore be said to be "valid". Our task here is to explore the emerging phenomena of the mind instead. In terms of the phenomena discussed in the last pages, it is the "agreement/disagreement" in terms of the distances between the selves that appears as a "mechanism" that uproots the groundings of our "sayings" and our everyday lives. Such uprooting might also allow for logics to deploy with a "foundation". It seems that already in ancient Greece there was an ontology of "what wisdom is" based on "accordance" and "agreement". For example, Heraclitus wrote:

> "To be temperate is the greatest virtue; and it is wisdom to speak the truth and to act according to nature with understanding. – Heraclitus."

Parmenides also wrote on what is "truly" true:

> "But judge by reasoning (argument) the hard-fought proof exhibited by me. – Parmenides."

Let us consider an example of such separation between "thinking" and the "concern that comes to us as a metaphysical need", and as if alien to our "true deep self", in as far as "we live alongside others". Let us start by saying that the fact that one speaks loudly and with strong convictions toward a "should" does not secure a grounding ground for the "should" or the "in order to" of the "living alongside others" as opposed to our "true deep should, need and in order to". That "others agree" and obviate such "is" and "need" is no proof of a lack of separation either. Let alone such "should" is here meant to speak for the "emergent phenomena" of our "true life and our true concern" as "close to the living alongside others". Such "should", "I" and "need" cannot be simply based on a "true deep self" and its deep "depth", "sincerity" or other. If anything, the "should", the "clarity" and "obviousness" of method in "our living alongside others" or the appealing to our "depth" of our "living with our deep self" might bury the emergent phenomena instead. In many cases "our deeper self" becomes the "task at hand" in that it is placed as a grounding ground to others. We are then to keep sight of the emergent phenomena rather than get ourselves into discussions regarding what a "true self is" as opposed to the self that we claim is not "us". In other words, self-evidence, obviousness, or clarity of outcome does not validate the matter that concerns this book in any way. The "emergent phenomena" that comes to the front is what concerns us. Even in the sense of emergency, it is the very sense of emergency that speaks of what "comes to the front" as "real everyday phenomena" regarding our "living alongside others" and our "deep self". This coming to the front might take place "buried" in the "ambiguity" of terms but can still be "sensed" through the veil of metaphysics. Let us take for example the "Discourse of the method" of Descartes. One might be tempted to conclude that "thinking" drives the author as "thinking" seems to "take priority" in the theme of the work[21]. His desire to "think" and appeal to "honest thinking" is then his "true deep self". Is it coincidence however that the book finishes with emergent everyday phenomena involving the living alongside others? The book finishes with:

> *"And I shall always hold myself more obliged to those whose favour enables me to enjoy uninterrupted leisure than to any who might offer me the most honourable employments in the world. – Descartes."*

The "true and deep self" that relates to the "thinking self" of Descartes is structurally equivalent, regarding the emergent phenomena of the mind, to the being "obliged to others self" of Descartes in the "living alongside others self" or the "talking to others". Such reference can also be turned upside down. We might even say that "thinking" could be the obfuscated "term" that Descartes exploited through the "living alongside others self" so to dedicate himself to the "true self" in the distance between his "selves". That is, our "telling others who we are so we can concern ourselves with what we truly are" appears as emergent "positive" phenomena of the mind. As the "positive" phenomena of the mind come to the front as a "task at hand" with a "toward", we are oriented and directing our minds and pointing at that which appears as "essential". The "being conscious of something", in as far as it comes to the front as that which "is", is to be "pushed aside" and relegated at any time. In this way, we have been "conscious" of what "is" as it has been "already mentioned". That is, what "is" has already been said so it is pushed to the side. Then, what "is" appeared "consciously" to then be "pushed aside" as what is otherwise "obviously" not the main task at hand. In our everyday lives we find ourselves telling each other: "We really need to talk about this, even though I know it's hard for you.", "You just don't want to see the truth because you are too self-involved, and you have your own plans.", "You just care about yourself.", and "positively", "I'm happy that we talked about this.", "This is something I always knew but I never managed to openly discuss it with you before.", "This has been a revelation but somehow I already knew it." In all the above cases we refer to some obfuscated and inconspicuous "deep self" that we find in our "talking to others" or in our "selves". Even if such "deep self" emerges in our sayings as we discuss it "deeply" we readily find ourselves "moving on to the task at hand" that comes next. This is what we mean here by "pushing aside" so to bring forth the "task at hand". The "talking" about our "true deep self" was still "a task at hand" that was then pushed for another "task at hand" to emerge. What is it then this task at hand that the mind leans toward? The answer to this question might as well reveal constitutive phenomena of the mind from the everydayness of "who" we are. Some have claimed the "deep reality" of our "task at hand" to be the "seeking of power". In his unfinished and last book "Will to power" Nietzsche claims that power leads us and is a fundamental "truth", i.e. will to power orients our minds. Whether will to power is or is not the "drive" of the mind is not our concern here however. That the "drive" is not our main concern readily clarifies that the "positive" phenomena of the mind cannot be reduced to "what we do" or "what drives us". That is, the mind "is not" a drive even if the mind constitutively seeks a drive or has one. If "will to power" is the grounding ground according to Nietzsche, such grounding appears structurally equivalent to the "happiness" or "peace of mind" as a foundation. That is, an uprooting ground. Heidegger said regarding the philosophy of Nietzsche:

> *"Nietzsche's metaphysics did not reach the fundamental question – Heidegger."*

Said plainly, ultimately, Nietzsche did not ask the question but "saw" an answer instead in his "depth". In this way, phenomena remained "veiled" by metaphysics. Some are now talking about "will to truth", "will to knowledge" and other as the "drive" of what we "are". We have made clear however that such "will" is not what we are "seeking" in our text, but rather, we describe the mind as what the mind "is". We also question "consciousness" as what possibly constitutes the mind. In that sense, the constitutive "positive" phenomena of the mind that emerge from the above writing relates to "seeking", "requiring" or "necessitating" a "drive" in the sense that the mind "seeks" to be driven. This drive might as well be "will to power" or what we term here our "task at hand". As we "are driven", we have "a task at hand in our everydayness" as what "is", and as what veils and protects as it comes to the front, what we claim that "truly is", i.e. our "deeper self" or our agreement with our "selves". Could we not reasonably argue that the "deep true self" of Descartes was "hiding" from us his "true concern" even by telling it to us as a "side concern pushed to the side" so he could dedicate himself to what "superficially concerns him"? The terms "deep" and "superficial" here appear not to be mocked, not as something to not be mocked either. Rather we are describing what comes proximally and for the most part in the inconspicuousness of the phenomena of the mind that just barely makes it to the surface. In this way, such terms are taken as what "obviously" comes but is otherwise not "clear" and might otherwise appear as "smoke". We are then to put ourselves in the position of the enquirer: The direction of the enquirer comes from the "directed" enquirer in that the "enquirer" faces the "everyday phenomena of life" and is already dealing with the phenomena of the mind in that the mind is already dealing with a "task at hand" and a "toward". Descartes thus presents us a phenomenon that is extremely subtle. That is, as we enquire the phenomena of the mind, the emergent phenomena that we face through our "living alongside others" is presented as metaphysically "superficial" while our "deep true self" seems to be the concern of study. In this way we "obviate" our "self" of our "living alongside others" as providing us with a "direction". If Nietzsche was not very mistaken in his seeing will to power as the drive, we could argue that will to power can be enforced more readily onto others by our "being ourselves and honest with others". This is because it is in our "living alongside others" that we can present more readily "who" we are. Descartes speaks of his approachable "everyday" life as a familiar term of "being with others" that others might "understand". The "drive" is then emerging from this "living alongside others" as it maintains a distance with the "self without others". That others also see who we are in our "living alongside us" gives us the possibility to "play games" with the distances of our "selves". Descartes should then be considered from his "living alongside others" and not "obviated" since it might "provide" the drive of his work and thinking. Furthermore, "obviation", "provision" and the discussing of agreement between the "selves" as we discuss the life and the "is" of others emerge as "positive" phenomena of the mind in that as we obviate, provide and discuss we see the "is" and the "need" of others. In any case, a simpler example that relates more "obviously" to this phenomenon could be a philosophy Professor abusing his power as he discusses power structures or social reality[22]. While this example appears as "obvious", it is not to be simply "obviated" and pushed to the side either. Moreover, we have already said that it might be the most "obvious" that obfuscates phenomena the most. That is, the most obvious might veil phenomena with obscure or unclear metaphysical terms. Similar everyday phenomena to that discussed in these chapters were discussed in "Being and time" by Heidegger. Amongst other he discusses "distantiality" that comes with "being with others", "inconspicuousness", "non-obstinacy", "idle talk", "curiosity" and the "indefiniteness of others as our concern" to be "ourselves with others". In summary, such turmoil of "words" and "complexity" of phenomena is not to be exploited to claim that there is an "obvious" grounding. The fixation for the grounding and its validity would just veil the emergent phenomena of the mind and displace the question of the mind.

## The uprooting ground, the violence of saying and the emergence of reality

Regarding the sciences, their directionality flows like a clock. From the planification of the "problem" a "toward" guides procedures securely to an "end". That the initial and final words of the storylines in structures of knowledge are robustly and strongly linked is in any case puzzling and speaks as much in favour of the firm and robust advances in some fields as of the positive accumulated knowledge in them. Sciences and other structures of knowledge move forward according to their directionality and from their ground, that being their major achievement and what supports them. That is, the value of these fields is the robustness and strength of their direction toward the essence of that which founded them provided they stick to the limits of their own directions and their grounds. We might call the flowing in their direction their own explanatory storyline, this time taking storyline as a positive explanatory object. The storylines of such fields we leave in this study untouched since our purpose is not to question their robustness. If what we explore in this book is related to any scientific field in any way, it is only done so to speak in favour of protecting their delimiting character and direction as their power. In this way we accept their robustness and support it in as far as they belong to their own field.

The phenomena that emerge when questioning the grounds of the "is", "need" and "function" in any explanatory storyline however, might still appear more as a leap than as a flow in terms of the structure and workings of the human mind as it concerns humans. This is because the foundation and direction of the storylines of structures of thought still appear as smoke if their limits are pushed where they were not meant to be pressured. That is, many times, that foundations totter does not speak of a deficiency in a structure, but rather, of the "coming off its limits" in the questions that a structure is many times erroneously made to confront. So why might a foundation totter even if the robustness of its method to an end is robust? The question itself might provide an answer, that is, "there is a method to an end". Taking this into account, foundations might totter because a structure of thought points in a direction but does not respond to its grounding as the grounding "uproots". Its direction cannot be made to come off its limits and outside its path to explore that which does not concern it since what does not concern it is alien to its path. In other words, the foundations of a structure of thought will be forced to totter as these are made to speak and answer to that which is not within their limits. This is what we term here a question that a structure of thought is erroneously made to confront; one cannot ask a question and follow a method that grants some answers and then ask these answers to ground a question that was never fundamentally involved. That a structure of thought fundamentally involves it all is otherwise tantamount to saying it involves nothing. That is, concerning it all is tantamount to being deficient in direction. For something to be robust in its method to an end, there must be an end. Having clarified that, the success of the sciences "positively" speaks of the directionality of sciences, their "accordance" to the mind and the "correct" method and approach of sciences in that "they delimit" their direction. A study in science "starts" where it is planned to start and "ends" where the study was planned to be taken whether successfully showing what was hoped it would show or not. In this way, what has direction is complete as its direction guides and grounds "toward" its "aim". When discussing "truth" and "Being" Parmenides might have been talking in these lines as he wrote:

> *"And remaining the same in the same place, it lies in itself and so it remains here steady: in fact the hard Necessity holds it in the bonds of the limit, shuts it around, since it is established that Being is complete: in fact it does not need anything; otherwise it would lack everything. – Parmenides"*

We might anyway dare to invoke what is not within the limits of what concerns a field by shattering its direction and foundations. Once one dares to place the direction of a structure of thought and its path as a grounding ground outside its limits, even the directions of the question totter and collapse. In this way, both the structure being questioned and the grounds of the question dissolve into a nothingness that can only succumb to the lack of grounding of a path that finds itself outside its limits. The question that shook it all is then "set free" to direct from a floating ground. A direction might "just emerge" as if from an "abyss". The feeling can be described as uncanniest or that which "loses all sites". We then become blind to any clear orientation and direction and the field can no longer speak robustly but just mumble. A mechanism for the dissolution of any structure of thought, that is, that makes it shake, totter and collapse, can in this way be said to involve the daring to come off its limits so to rise above them. In as far as we are "outside" its limits however, we are not "referring" to it and it is "ourselves" that lie outside it, not otherwise. In this way, the field, structure of thought or scientific method is now not talking about itself in our "saying". It is then our question that "remains" alien to it while the structure is "untouched". In the same tragedy of Sophocles that we quoted, he wrote:

> *"Rising high over the site, losing the site is he for whom what is not, is, always, for the sake of daring –* Sophocles.*"*

It is this "daring" that is always a possibility in our "saying" as we "see" the "is" and the "real". The daring itself is what takes us to other. As we dare, we build, we "see" other and we "bring into existence" whether we saw "correctly" or not. We quote some famous lines that Frederik Nietzsche wrote about 100 years ago:

> *"Beware that, when fighting monsters, you yourself do not become a monster... for when you gaze long into the abyss. The abyss gazes also into you. – Nietzsche."*

> *"Mathematics would certainly have not come into existence if one had known from the beginning that there was in nature no exactly straight line, no actual circle, no absolute magnitude. – Nietzsche."*

This takes us to another question. How and why do we "say" even if we might claim that "nothing is", that "reality is relative", that there are only "opinions" or that while we "see" this, we also "see" other? In the case of a dissolving ontology, the conceiving of any ontology as possible, or even the undertaking of one which is "truly real" - in each case at hand, and to each of us legitimately - is facilitated simply because it can. In this way, an underlying ontology might prevail and direct toward that "which should be", even if ambiguously. Such ontology directs in the form of an ungrounded ontology in that the grounding of the ground might not even be questioned or mentioned. This is the phenomenon of "uprooting". The uprooting ground might not be considered in that it might merely pass unseen or unthought, or simply missed or disregarded as obvious. This takes us back to the tragedy of Sophocles, Heraclitus and the "fleeing" from metaphysics. Ontologies that direct as if "ways of life" are accepted as an "obvious" possibility and act by dictating or assuming what we and our needs are. These ontologies settle a direction or even multiple directions in the name of "truth", "reality", "logics" or other metaphysically ungraspable terms and are, in any case, presumed as these things "which of course should dictate" what we "ought to be" and the "direction that we must follow" to an "end". The so-called end is otherwise rarely properly mentioned, let alone explored limitlessly without restriction. One might otherwise "choose to be so and so" because of the concept of freedom of choice. We say, "there is freedom of choice". One might simply not hear but say because of the justice of freedom of speech. We say, "I say because I am free to speak". Any of these sentences is otherwise easily negated by us or others as we say, argue and confront. In front of such sentences violently presented as the placing of a ground that uproots, one becomes speechless and left astounded, as the bottomless ground that they present, as well as their uprooting upwards, manifests and unfolds in front of us as a "happening". This is a form of the "uncanny" placing with violence that uproots an ungrounded ground that is unique to humans. The "uprooting" in sayings can be felt at any time as we ask for advice for example. Advice comes in the form of a direction that emerges and directs by already conforming to itself. The more solid the advice, the more it conforms toward its path from its placing. Sophocles wrote in the same tragedy:

> *"Manifold is the uncanny, yet nothing uncannier than man bestirs itself, rising up beyond him. - Sophocles."*

The dissolving of ontologies resonates in each corner and appears ever more as smoke. That one dares to ask and come off limits in favour of challenging questions, directions and the positioning of a structure of thought, or even the most fundamental fields of science, is visible in society in all its ambits. We dare to confront and impose as we also dare to say.

If what we say is imposed by our saying however, are not things what they are as far as they are said? A sign of the dissolving of ontologies to mere opinions made of words that dissolve as smoke, as well as of the values fabricated with opinions, can be noticed in the losing of any explanatory power as the grounding of it all becomes ungraspable the more one questions its groundings. The deepest and most "sacred" foundations are thus seen as "an opinion" and challenged as to their validity and direction. We seem to speak of what we do not know, yet, we dare to "say". We hear people in all ambits of life confronting the "lack of normality" or the "relative" value of "normality" or simply the meaningless meaning of speaking of what is "normal", "real" or "true". We also confront experts in what they say and claim they "don't know". One otherwise appeals to what is real when one encounters "real" problems in life by invoking the correspondence of what is said to a "true reality". Only when the "real" problems of life come forth, there is a clearing that silences the relativizing and trivializing of the concepts and terms that otherwise appeared as smoke. In this way, from the "meaningless" chattering of the everyday life as an otherwise concerning chat, one comes to "the true matter at hand". At this point there is "truth" and "obviousness" in the "toward". This is found even in our "looking for experts" as we need to know what "is" and the what of what we "need". We might say: "I need food so I'm going to the shop later." or "The car broke so I need a good mechanic." Other times we just "need expert advice". As we go back to rest or back to our everyday form of chatter, we might "go back" to the relativity and appearance of values as mere opinions as the relativity of what is "true" manifests unequivocally. Metaphysical terms are then replaced by others that appear as equally ambiguous and as if lacking any ground or directionality. In these circumstances, as words come out, even if there is no "is", there is "saying" that speaks of what "is". In such conditions, "depth" comes to "meet" us in a very different way compared to how we encounter it when "facing" our "true realities".

The uprooting or "building up" of a structure of thought, a philosophy or metaphysics of life in terms of words, as far as they are just mentioned recklessly, simply obviated or in the oblivion as a foundation, or said as what "is", is what we term here the ungrounded ground or the ground that is otherwise ungrounded. From "saying" occurring as a "happening", the "is" uproots and grounds itself upward toward what is being "said". Structurally and to the mind, all uprooting grounds are the same. Uprooting grounds many times do not even appear as ungrounded but just obviated as "opinions", "relative realities" or even "truths" that do not explain it all or simply appear as "false" or as "meaningless" terms that lack an anchoring to "reality". We might say: "It's all relative so there is no point to argue." or "Don't you see that that is just your point of view?". We might also claim that "there are many points of view but only one reality." - presumably we "see" now what reality "is". In any case all these sentences come as a violent "placing" of words that "say". Only as the distance between our "self" that is "concerned" with our "real life" and our "living alongside others unattending the reality of our lives" manifests, there are "sayings" and "sayings". This distance does not need to include our "true deep self" or other selves. There are "sayings" and "sayings" in as far as there is a "distance" between selves or a "distance" between us and others. As we discussed in the previous chapters, these distances are measured by the "is" and "need" at hand that emerge as "we live". Sophocles follows in the tragedy regarding the rising high over the site:

> *"Rising high over the site, losing the site is he for whom what is not, is, always, for the sake of daring. Let him not become a companion at my hearth, nor let my knowing share the delusions of the one who works such deeds. – Sophocles."*

One might otherwise dare to live "without direction" or "fundamental judgment" as if in a chaotic state of mind, or even more intriguingly, in the possibility of the ungrounded in terms of, and as far as, that which "ought to be" takes place as that which is just said when one says it. As if we were "our own God" following our whim. The placing of words with violence that opens a "path" to be travelled occurs as a "happening" that places the human as the "God". In the same tragedy Sophocles wrote:

> *"Between the ordinance of the earth and the gods' sworn dispensation he fares[1]. – Sophocles."*

This is another form of the "uncanniest" expression of humanity as Sophocles puts it. Uncanny in that it comes as a violent placing.

In the presence of ontological "chaos", accepting a direction at hand appears as a complex phenomenon "intellectually" in that one must choose something from apparently nothing. One must "ground" the "ungroundable". On the other hand, the "living our lives" always presents an "is", "need" and a

---

[1] We could translate fare as "take their own direction"

"toward" at hand as one lives that presents itself in front of us. The uprooting here might appear to us even through the "logics" of "needing" to have something to "hold on to" since with "nothing" one "simply loses the mind" or "cannot cope with life itself". Such "logics" have nothing to do with textbook logics. Here, we refer to the "ambiguity" of the "logics" that we appeal to in our everyday life as an "obvious" thing that we of course "need". We might say to one another: "You need to hold onto something." or "You need to focus on something.". When one does not even know what to do next, "nothing" appears as an option, as one might say: "You just need a rest. Take it and enjoy it." In this way, the possibility of the "obviousness" of an option that comes delivered at hand might even be "willed", "wished" or "hoped" as "nothing". That is, there is appeasing even through "nothing" as the "is". Appeasing mostly when there is an "is" even if that is "is" "nothing". One might say "I wish I knew what I feel" or "I wish I knew what I ought to do with my life". In our everyday lives we also encounter many moments when one is simply lost regarding things that also appear as "floating" phenomena regarding "anything or any task at hand" that is otherwise "unimportant". It always remains unimportant if one "says" it is "unimportant". For example, one might say: "Do you feel like going out? I'm asking because I don't know what to do." or "I don't know if I should go out for dinner". The emerging phenomena of the mind here is again a "seeking" of a direction. Through the phenomena of "seeking" a direction a "true reality" that is unambiguous, even if only as one "says so", emerges as a possibility again as a "because I say so". This happens no matter how strongly or robustly one "breaks" or exposes the ungrounding of any structure of thought or metaphysical value in the daily life of casual chatting regarding that which is otherwise taken to be a "deep" concern. The same happens with any intellectual abstraction of the "is" no matter how profound. Even if we could prove theoretically that any "is" is ultimately empty and does not mean anything, we would still continuously deal with the "is" and the "need" at hand as we live. We can now quote the sentence of Heraclitus that was already quoted in the introduction with a new view to it:

> *"For they turn their backs on that with which they traffic the most, λόγος, and what they run into every day appears alien to them. – Heraclitus."*

As a possibility inherent to the directionality of the mind one might "break from all metaphysics" by fully falling into "nothingness" as an uprooting ground. "Nothingness" might also appear as an option as we are just "saturated" with ourselves, our "is", our "need" and our "task at hand" and we "just can't take it anymore". Even though one "needs" to take it anyway, the "seeking" of the mind and its "concern" with what "is" and what is "needed" seems to "need" a rest from "needing". We might say to each other: "You need to take a rest." or "Don't push yourself o much. You need to take care of yourself." While such falling into "nothingness" seems like a "fall" however, there are even higher ranks in the "falling" of the mind. We could call the full falling of the mind the "terrible", the "dreadful" and the "disorienting" in that even the inherent directionality of the mind is at stake, i.e. "one is losing oneself fully in all respects." After breaking it all fully, one might be left in the presence of nothingness as if glancing at the "abyss" referred to by Nietzsche above. What is it that is left after falling into the "abyss"? As long as one "lives", an effective "is" still emerges. That is, soon enough, one might "move forward" toward the "real" needs of life and thus carry on with it by "pushing" philosophies aside so to confront the taking care of that which is meaningful, that is, "the real need". The coming of the "is" might happen even if we say to ourselves "I've had enough" and even when we "simply forget it all and just move on." In this way we still "know". The "what" of that which is "truly real" always emerges as what "is" even from the total collapse of the foundations of metaphysics as one lives. Nietzsche might have termed this the "depth of the body" over the emptiness or groundlessness of metaphysics. If metaphysics speaks of "nothing" then the "need" is in the body, that is, in what will support our "moving on" with life. In Thus Spoke Zarathustra he wrote:

> *""I", you say, and are proud of the word. But greater is that in which you do not wish to have faith – your body and its great reason: that does not say "I", but does "I" … There is more reason in your body than in your best wisdom. – Nietzsche."*

In principle, the "knowing" of the "pressuring need" would then provide a ground that would direct us toward a "toward", no matter how ambiguously or groundlessly. These sentences might otherwise be clarified as follows: with the possibility of an "option" that is "logical", "true" or other, no matter what such logics, truth or reality might be, a path opens up that can act as a guide to "straighten up" our lives into that "which they should be". The foundation is the "straightening up" of our life itself. For example, by following the "advice" of how the "mechanisms" of life work, i.e. biology, neuroscience or other, and how the knowing of such mechanisms might "help" us in life, we are being guided by a "straightening up" of our lives. The phenomena accompanying the appearance of this guidance that orients and directs us into that which "we should be" however, remains as unclear and ambiguous after a logical explanation is given, whether in terms of neuroscience or self-help books offering advice, as it was before. How is this phenomenon relevant to the mind and to the "is" of the mind"? Even in the breaking up of any metaphysics or structure of thought one simply places in front of them a path even if ambiguously grounded. That path might be our "everyday life itself" as we "live it". The mind keeps dealing with an "is" at hand through such path. Such path appears to us as "our reality" and as that which is "truly real" as it truly directs our lives that come with our placing. That we question such paths appears as a distance between the different forms of "is" and "need" of our "selves". In this way, the phenomena of the "appearance" of the "straightening up" of "our lives" as a grounding ground remains as elusive and unarticulated as the "carrying on" with our lives after the dissolution of any values. Again, what is this to do with the phenomena of the mind? Irrespectively of the lack of a "reasoned" ground that does not involve formal contradictions, a form of "reality" always emerges as a path as we live. This path might present itself very clearly and with a defined "toward" and "in order to" or not so clearly. This "positive" phenomenon appears persistently and stubbornly no matter how strongly the view of the "emptiness" of metaphysics or this "deeper" meaning of life (or body) is not supported. Since the concern of this work is the emergence of "positive" phenomena of the mind, it is not the validity of the foundation of "metaphysics" itself that is directly at stake. Instead, it is the emergence of a "path" in our everyday lives that we take as an emergent "positive" phenomenon of the mind. On the other hand, the phenomena of concern with metaphysics, or the lack of "grounding" of metaphysics, also involves the mind and its emerging phenomena in a different way. Namely, the tendency of pushing metaphysics aside when facing what appears as "real and true" phenomena at hand in real life is an emergent "positive" phenomenon of the mind. Furthermore, the stubborn appearance of the "is" and the "need" at hand as we live, in any form and from any type of ground, even if ungrounded or uprooting, emerges also as "positive" phenomena.

There is a final theme worth mentioning here that relates to the "reorientation of the mind". That is, we will just "move on with life" as there is "pressure" in life toward a "toward". Nevertheless, a different "toward" might still come. Put in the form of a question: how come we sometimes change our minds regarding the "is" and the "need" at hand of even our "true deep selves"? This happens as a possibility where at any time we might open up to a new "reality" that we never saw before. Such opening up might take place in time or as a shock. A shock occurs as a realization of that which was always "present in front of us" but was never before "acknowledged as such" as we just realize it as a vital reality and as a shock. It was always in front of us in as far as it concerns our lives and we are always dealing with our lives. Vital in that it presents itself as essential to the grounding of our lives. It might also present itself as vital in that it might lay in front of us an uprooting ground that is groundless at bottom. This "uprooting ground" emerges as the "is" of our lives. This opening up might also relate to the flow of distances between our "living alongside others self", our "true deep self" or our "ambiguously defined self" as these "selves" "see" the other "selves" and measure themselves against each other. In the same way that looking at the past one always detects what one missed, one realizes what was missed with any shock of violence that life puts in front of us. This is another way in which one might take a glance at the "ungrounded" and uprooting of the ground. As we "see" such uprooting, the "abyss" manifests in front of us. That stimulants, meditation, drugs, self-help books, philosophy or other manifest as a seductive orienting path that will orient us, is as plausible as the multiplicity of the directing schools that exist. Again, the recurring appearance of experiencing the "abyss" is indicative of the stubbornness of the phenomenon of the "shock" and the new "realization" of what "is". We might feel "truly shocked" or something might "change our minds altogether." An experience might "change the way we see things fully." We might even tell each other that we "need" to expand our "reality" by "seeing other." The seeing other of the "true shock" however doesn't come as a simple "change of mind" but as a "shattering" or "collapsing". As humans live, humans "see" and "change" their minds. In the case of the shock, the emergence of the "true reality" that we see in the phenomena that forms part of our everyday lives might bridge a gap between the "deep" metaphysics that are not "real" and our "true life" that confronts metaphysics. That is, while both the "true reality" of our lives and the "deep and empty" metaphysics, that might otherwise appear as if diluting, are groundless at bottom, in as far as they uproot, these can link and bridge in the emergence of the shock. At this point we witness the "abyss" and the "is" and "need" of our "selves", as well as the "distances" between the "is" and "need" of our different "selves", change us altogether.

## The leaning toward what "is" still concealed

In the previous chapter we said that directions, logics and truths are there for us "to take". This availability suggests that precedence lies always in the possibility of "orienting" oneself toward "that which comes". This happenes as if living life facilitates or even seeks the possibility of "grasping" this or that as "what is" our actual path. We seem to "see" and "know" as we live our everyday lives. This is the positive phenomenon that came forth as a "path that always comes to orient us" as we set to live. We further say that through our everyday lives, shocks of life or other, and always in some occasions, one discovers something that was there but was otherwise "not seen" before. That is, that "one does not see" does not imply that "something is not there in front of oneself", but rather, that "what could otherwise be" remains "as if hidden or concealed" until "acknowledged" as present. Before acknowledging it, it appeared as just a "semblance" in as far as it was "concealed", or it was simple "unseen". One might otherwise follow a path without unambiguously acknowledging what one sees but still see something. In this way, even when we are already "oriented toward a path" or we already "see", there is always the possibility to "see other" that also "is" but that in our "seeing already" or our "lack of seeing" we cannot come to see. To "see" that which "is" but cannot "be seen", one must "dare" to lean toward it so to "see". One must "dare" to step into the path that "is there" for us to follow while at the same time appears as if "it is not" there. Does not the possibility of "not seeing" what is present in front of us and "having to risk leaning toward seeing it" to "see it" present itself as a risk in our everyday lives? Heraclitus wrote:

> *"If you do not expect the unexpected, you will not find it, for it is too difficult to seek out. – Heraclitus."*

The risk of the "possible path ahead" might present to us the "menace" of "deception" that always lies there as a possibility, not only in the "liar" that we mentioned above regarding what Nietzsche said about premeditated lying, but also as an "unknown" that might otherwise come as if "unnoticed by all". Such "daring to see" is a risk that is continuously menacing our stability and the direction of our minds. That risk is always there, as a menace, but also as a possibility to see what "truly is" in front of us so to "reject" what maybe "is not" but now "seems to be" what (deceptively) "is". This possibility to see by leaning toward that which is already in front of us also acts as a sign in our theme and as a signal toward a call.

Humans seem to always be exposed to this "knowing" but otherwise "not knowing fully" or to an ambiguously "known" that might otherwise "deceive". The possibility to "see better" or "other" is there for us as a "dare". Such situation of "expectation", "ambiguity" or otherwise "anguish", in that one tends to want to be sure to know, or the "need" to know itself, also emerge as positive phenomena of the mind. To Heraclitus, knowing that all is and is not "is" wisdom in that it is the measure of all things and "sees" all things the same. The "being and not being" is a common theme in Heraclitus and also in Parmenides, maybe two of the pillars of ancient pre-Socratic Greece. We give an example here to bring to familiarity what such "wisdom" might be. For this we will use an analogy to the following saying of Heraclitus:

> *"No one of all whose discourses I have heard has arrived at this result: the recognition that wisdom is apart from all other things. - Heraclitus."*

*Sergio Santos, Matteo Chiesa and Maritsa Kissamitaki.*

The analogy goes as follows:

> *"As we are to build a car, we are to do all the things that are required so to build it. On the other hand, we might find ourselves at any point wondering what we should do next even if we know how to do it all. In as far as we should do the full car, what we do next doesn't matter. It would matter only if our goal was to build more efficiently and one thing was to be built before the other. In as far as there is all to do however, it doesn't really matter what we do provided we do it all. So, there is no point to be uncertain about what to do next because we know that what is required is to build the whole car. Knowing that doing one thing or another will take us to building the full car all the same is wisdom. Whereas knowing how to do one thing regarding the building itself even if we know how to build all parts and we eventually manage to build the full car is just knowing things."*

How does the analogy above relate to being and not being and "seeing" and "not seeing" what "is"? By having the possibility to see or not see, humans are and are not, humans might dare to step or might not, they might attempt to see other or see already what is seen. So, it is as if we are many times "about to attempt stepping into a path" that otherwise "might not be what we think it is" or stay in the path that we think "it is what we think it is". Heraclitus wrote:

> *"We both step and do not step in the same rivers. We are and are not. - Heraclitus"*

Let us interpret the above sayings of Heraclitus in as far as one can seem to step into a given direction but might otherwise appear as if somehow stepping into another in terms of what is feared. Let us start by exploring how that one "can otherwise see now" what "one could not see before" is a threat and a source of deception in that "one can always see" provided "one is already predisposed to see". The seeing "a path" is always there as a possibility. This possibility "is there" as a daring. One might very strongly "see" what "truly" is. On the other hand, while by "seeing" strongly one might be robustly grounded and moving into a "path" that one "sees", another path might "present itself as a possibility". The presenting of another path itself acts as a source of "tottering" and "shaking" of our path. The stronger the "seeing" the more robustly we hold onto what "is" as it holds us back and grounds us. In this way one is firmly grounded and set. It is otherwise only when what we "see" totters or sways that one might "dare" to "see" or otherwise find themselves in a position of "leaning toward other". If we saw other however, what we get to "see" already "was". As one "sees" in a given direction, things "are", and a direction is set. Such workings of the "seeing" what things are as a whole rather than "seeing" the something of a particular thing only, is in this way related to the saying of Heraclitus above and the analogy that we referred to. That is, as we see "this" we can also see "that" as long as things "are" and we "see" them as a whole of what "is". We can refer this seeing the whole to the analogy of "seeing" how to "build" a whole car. Parmenides wrote:

> *"For now it is, all at once, a continuous one. For what kind of origin for it wilt thou look for? – Parmenides."*

The possibility of, or in any case the possibility to "seek", another direction poses the human in front of the "abyss" twice. First, in that "what is not seen" could otherwise be that "which will truly orient us" and "hold us" as who we are in a way that we are not "deceiving ourselves". Otherwise it might "orient us" into a deception of what "it is not" and so it will orient us into a "disorientation". This symbolizes the risk, dare and menace of "seeing" what is "not" as much as the possibility to see what truly "is". In any case, to see, one must "dare". We call this daring an attempt to "attend" that which calls us. Second, "once seen" an orientation and a direction might guide us in a way that it allows us to place in front of us and in front of others "what is" as opposed to what "is not" in as far as we see it. In that we see it, but others might not, we might appear to others as "the one that does not see", that is, the "unconscious". Others might appear to us as "the ones that do not see", that is, the "unconscious". As we step directed onto our path "we see our path" in front of us, while our path might or might not "be seen by others". The "path" of others appears as the "path that deceives" but might otherwise "be". We are always facing a sway between the "conscious" and the "unconscious" or the "seeing" and the "not seeing". It always comes as a shock when someone says to us: "Don't you see that you are wrong?" or "I can't believe that you don't see!". Facing the "unconscious", or otherwise the possibility of the "unconscious" to appear anytime in front of us, as the "dreadful" and "uncanny", appears as a phenomenon in our everyday lives as a possibility. This possibility of facing the "unconscious" at any time emerges as a "positive" phenomenon of the mind. The "unconscious" might appear as the "unconscious" only deceptively in that the "unconscious" remains unconscious provided we don't dare to "see". This possibility of the "unconscious" to actually "see" what we do not "see" and therefore that we are "deceived" ourselves instead, that is, that we are the "unconscious", also appears as a phenomenon in our everyday lives as a possibility. As we "see" what we are "we are what we are" but we also might not "see". Sometimes we say: "I totally ruined my life! I'm lost." or "What I did today was great! I am invincible.". As we "see" the directionality of the mind "directs" us. What comes to the front "is" and so we are that which we "see" (think).

Parmenides wrote in his fragment on truth:

*"... in fact it is the same to think and to be. – Parmenides."*

As we "dare to see" what we "are not" as we don't "see it", we "are" in the condition of concealed until revealed as we "see" it. So, we are what we are not, and we are not what we are. This being and not being might phenomenally appear as a sway of being and not being to the mind. On the other hand, as we "see" what "is", what is not "is not" and cannot even be expressed. As we cannot "express" how could logics and arguments even make sense? Arguments and logics would appear, as Heraclitus said, as barks. Parmenides also wrote:

*"I teach you that this is an entirely unknown way; neither in fact you could know the Non-Being (in fact it is impossible) nor you could express it. – Parmenides."*

This type of phenomenon stubbornly manifests in our everyday lives as a riddle of language and as a riddle of what we "truly" are. We might say the same about all that "is". In this way, the phenomenon of "reality" or "truth" "appearing" as "real" to humans, but that might otherwise shake or totter to then allow to envisage another "reality" or "truth" as "real", emerges as a "positive" phenomenon of the mind. We always find ourselves facing the possibility to see or not see what is real or deceptive. What we "see" however, "is" always. That this phenomenon grounds the standard concepts of "truth" and "real" as relative or as "mere opinions" appears as ambiguously as such claim appears to be fraudulent, i.e. a treachery at bottom. The more fraudulent as the terms "truth" and "real" are the most "sacredly" guarded in our everyday lives in what guides us even as they dissolve. Society exploits these words continuously in an "attempt" to ground actions toward that which "is" and "ought to be". In the middle of this turmoil of words new technologies such as AI and new laws are set to establish and come upon us.

## The directionality of the mind

We present a description of the mind in terms of the mind as what orients us. Our theme is descriptive in that it phenomenally presents the "what" of the mind as the "mind" appears as a phenomenon that we, in all cases and always, are already acquainted with in a very direct fashion. The object of this book is the mind in that the mind is that which we already know and own as our own as that which guides us and orients us. Even in the lack of guidance and orientation the mind presents itself as that which might get us back onto a track. In this way we describe the mind as "the mind of humans" in that humans use their minds to "see the world" in which they live in and in that with the mind humans orient themselves in the world by attending to that which presents itself and to them as essential. Humans might attend to what presents itself as such in whatever orientation it assumes, ambiguously or not, or might otherwise miss it or simply ignore the call to attend. The phenomenon of attending is not one where the mind might merely take that which was outside the mind and built itself up as a thought as if outside of us or as if something got inside of us and then built itself as in parts. But rather, attending is a process in which the building up of the orientation always belongs to the orienting of the mind as much as to that which orients it.

The mind orients us as we lean toward that which comes to orient us. We strengthen up the orientation as we lean toward it and simultaneously strengthen or weaken the "is" of who we are as we either accept or confront the orientation of other/s. Similarly, others also orient or disorient themselves through our orientation as we "say" and "listen". In that way, we live in a world that orients us as we orient it. That with the mind we orient ourselves is not to be taken as "the mind" alone "perceives" apart from the body or other organs. The mind here is rather taken as a whole of that which "orients us" in the phenomenon of "orientation" as such. In this way, this book is not about sensorial functions or interfaces that otherwise affect a factual orientation, emotion, or other mechanisms in the brain that feedback from one place to another, but rather, our theme is about the possibility of assuming an "orientation" in the world as such, or otherwise not assuming it. The mechanisms of perception in terms of their function belong to other fields that are suited for the task. Thus, the orientation is not discussed here in terms "of that which affects us" in the sense that there might be "something outside us" in the world or "something inside us" in our bodies that interacts with us as an "interface" that is to be found somewhere. The assuming of an orientation is rather taken as that which guides us in the way of a call that calls for attention or that calls to be attended in as far as it comes to the front as what "is". In summary, whether changing physical parts of the body or brain, modifying these, varying concentrations of a substance or other, might change perception is not what we seek to discuss here since those are mechanisms and not phenomena of the mind as sought here. Many fields are well founded and suited for that kind of study. Their reach is also discussed in the next section. On the other hand, such believing that through perception we know things is nothing new. Heraclitus already wrote:

> *"If happiness was the pleasures of the body, we ought to call cattle happy when they find a patch of vetch. – Heraclitus."*

*"If all things became smoke, the nose could tell them apart. - Heraclitus."*

As we allow ourselves to be oriented, we are to lean toward that which calls. One might otherwise be "ambiguously" oriented as if partially "oriented". Here, that an orientation appears as ambiguous or unclear in that it has not been fully clarified as to the "what" of that which is orienting is not considered a deficiency of the inherent directionality of the mind. Neither is considered a deficiency the ignoring of what presents itself as essential, nor the lack of focus, concentration or motivation for a task at hand. In this sense, the invitation to exploring the mind and thinking in this book is not an invitation to question the "for what" or the "in order to" of the guiding of the mind toward a "where" or an "end" that fulfills an "in order to". But rather, and if anything, we seek to describe how the workings of the mind facilitate phenomenal directions of the mind such as those that reach a "for what" or an "in order to" in terms of the directionality of the mind. The mind can otherwise neglect or miss a possible object of thought, orientation or call, or even more strongly, fully reject it. The discussion of the "why" and the "for what" this is so is not the theme that concerns us since such themes require a "direction" and are already the theme of many fields of research. That the structure of the mind emerges as inherent directionality and orientability is our theme.

## The mind, thinking and the sciences

The mind is here differentiated from an "intelligent" entity that predicts. The mind is in that sense not comparable to "an intelligent entity" no matter how "intelligent" this entity is in predicting or how efficiently it works, reasons, or debates. A predicting device will always be deficient in "seeing the world" and orienting itself in the world as a human as long as the predicting device is already conforming to the task of "predicting" this or that. This is so even if the prediction agrees with what humans would otherwise predict. A predictive device will miss the operations of the mind provided "the listening to a call" and the standing in front of the "abyss" and facing its "menacing" glance is missed. The same could be said about "optimizing", "searching", "recognizing", "classifying" algorithms or "AI assistants". This is so irrespective of whether such prediction, classification or other is in "true" agreement with a set of statements and also irrespective of how much these statements are in correspondence with a "true reality". That is, the outcome of the device being "true" or "correct" in terms of this or that is not what is at stake. Here we do not refer to "truth" or "correct" in that one might have a set of possibilities out of which one "is the correct one" while the others are not. It is also not the case that we refer to "relative" points of view in that "there is no correct one" or even in that there might be inconsistencies in terms of whether one can be said to be correct. It is also not the theme of this book to disqualify or discredit such forms of artificial intelligence or machine learning algorithms that reach their goals. Intelligent algorithms are advancing the fields of science and technology and "achieving their specific goals" which can coincide with predicting, classifying or other. Such set of algorithms and platforms for AI techniques are successfully advancing toward their respective targets which are, in any case, validated in most respects.

Our theme here, in the above sense, is not a negative critique toward AI, science, or any algorithm and it certainly cannot be. This is so because the matter that is being discussed here can be grasped in the sciences only, and in any case, in that science already has a direction. Thus, that AI entities can "reason" or be "intelligent" is sustained in a "toward what" of a path that is "guided" in a very specific way and in a very peculiar direction. For example, algorithms are "guided" toward optimization, stability or even the simulation of freedom or free will. Technology might be guided toward the building of equipment that is fast and robust. Thus, thinking, in the sense of what is described in this book, relates to the sciences only in that sciences must be, and because of the way in which they operate they are, unconscious to other than the call that is already dictated. This is moreover and precisely the "positive" character of the sciences and the one that provides them with their characteristic robustness. We are at this point in a position to make a statement regarding AI techniques and machine learning in general:

> *"It is precisely that AI and machine learning techniques have*
> *a path that they follow, delimited to that which makes them*

*what they are, that allows them to advance toward their
goals. Let that be "optimizing", "classifying", "simulating
free will" or other. Furthermore, the clearer and the more
delimited the path and direction, the clearer and more robust
the advances. If anything, sciences need to clarify the matter
for which they speak and delimit it in their method"*

The sentences above are nothing new to science in that sciences always
tend toward their own delimited direction and structure. Furthermore, it
is the owning of the foundation of such directionality that provides them
with their peculiar essence in a way that they can be called "sciences". In
the same sense AI and machine learning techniques can follow and should
follow their path in accord with their directiveness, that is, in as far as they
are already on their way toward their path. With such introduction to what
this book is in terms of how it differentiates from the sciences and even
AI techniques we are further in a position to quote Heidegger regarding
the sciences:

*"… science itself does not think, and cannot think – which
is its good fortune, here meaning the assurance of its own
appointed course… even though science always and in its own
fashion has to do with thinking - Heidegger."*

The way in which science has to do with thinking is revealed in the next
sentence:

*"The fashion that relates science to thinking is genuine and
fruitful only after the gulf - or gap- has become visible that
lies between thinking and the sciences. The gap - between
thinking and the sciences - is unbridgeable - Heidegger."*

In other words, there is no bridge between the sciences and thinking, i.e.
one cannot claim to genuinely commit to thinking once the scientific path
is taken in its specific scientific way. Since there is no bridge, to reach the
sciences from thinking one needs to "leap", i.e. there is "only a leap" but
not a bridge. Since the "sciences have already heard the call" and follow
their direction, sciences and the affairs of this book are related only in

that "sciences" are a limiting paradigm of a call that already conforms to a guidance. To be a scientist, one must conform with the sciences. Today there is the "danger" in the sciences that some want to "think" them "pseudo scientifically". In that pseudoscientific "thinking" wants to "tell" the sciences their path and how these should "operate", science itself can collapse. The attacks to the sciences typically come from those who attack them by invoking their incapacity to respond to all that lies outside the limits of science. Such attacks are simply erroneous and misguiding and speak of other than science. Pointing at "that" they want to modify "this". Such attacks also find themselves in a position where, to "see" the "what" and the "toward" of science, they must leap. They must leap because they must "reorient" for one to see the other. Rather than leaping however, they follow a path that does not concern the sciences. Their path is alien to the sciences and thus speaks of "other" in a way that a conversation between the two would turn only into barks at most. In summary, one can only point at the "wrong doing" of the sciences where one sees that the sciences do not "follow" themselves, that is, where one believes that they get "off track" and outside their path. What are these pseudo sciences and why do we call them pseudo sciences? We call them pseudo sciences in that they "speak" as if "doing science" but do "no science". Any scientific attack that behaves in this way is not "attacking" the foundations of science so to reinforce them, but rather, such attack is redirecting science toward that which science is not. The metaphysical chaos that surrounds media, politics, ethics, our own "selves" and institutions might be reinforcing the dangerous and sometimes mischievous attacks on science. In the same sense, our theme here is the phenomena of the mind in a way that we cannot "attack" the sciences and we most definitely do not do so. This is because our issue is not its concern in the same way that the concern of the sciences is not ours.

# The Object of The Mind

## The mind as what we already know

That we are the rational being that thinks rests upon the grounds of thinking in as far as we can lean toward and think about what is, beforehand and before we dedicate ourselves to, concealed. Humans are the rational being that speaks and thinks. Yet we do not know how we do it and have to learn about what it means before we can teach robots or any other intelligent entities including ourselves. Similar statements were already placed by Heidegger in his writings regarding the question "*What Is Called Thinking?*". In any case, we formally question humans as they think:

*How can the rational being that speaks and thinks need to learn what speaking and thinking means?*

That humans speak but do not know how might already give us to think about. We can start by arguing that we do think and that the matter of thinking is relevant to the mind. The matter of thinking is as relevant now as it has always been and even more in many respects. Some of the aspects of thinking that make it a very relevant topic today relate to dramatic scientific advances. Through scientific breakthroughs we are finding ways to monitor the mechanisms that regulate brain activity[23] and manipulate them[24]. Manipulation of the brain to regulate activity is further moving from a simplistic view of taking a pill to an end to full brain manipulation and understanding[25]. Even the relationships between our everyday activity, social status and mental state are being deciphered in terms of the molecular mechanisms involved with our genetics and epigenetics[26]. New social phenomena such as social media is being considered by neuroscience and the social sciences as affecting our cognition[27]. The capacity to interact with virtual characters and identify with them, for example in video games, is showing us how complex the mechanisms of association in the brain are and how complex finding correlations might be[28]. There are also many books dedicated exclusively to explaining how the mechanisms of the brain work both academically[29] and to educate people regarding what the brain is and how it affects the perception of who we are[30]. These books and research dedicate much of their work to explaining how we think and perceive and take thinking as a given fact of what we do, and rightly so. Even if we can think however, how does any thought come about? This question does not concern the how in as far as the molecular mechanism or even the how of the higher functions of the brain. Again, we are questioning the emergence of the phenomena instead. Taking this consideration into account, is there a way of thinking about a matter that is more essential or valid than another? In discussing the mind, thinking and the matters of thinking seem to come as a natural departing point for exploring thought. Thought has brought about powerful and profound discoveries. Humans have brought thinking to the limit in all fields of science, technology and humanities. Humanity has developed, exploiting even the subtlest details and information, theories that require meticulous and sharp thinking. For example, cosmic blackbody radiation has been found to provide information about the beginnings of the universe, its current expansion and the conditions required at the decoupling time when the Big Bang took place. Humanity has discovered the code of life in DNA and through the Human Genome Project "identified and mapped all of the of the human genome from both a physical and a functional standpoint". These achievements came by developing with wit, intelligence and brightness the most sophisticated instrumentation for manipulating and sequencing molecules that are, on the other hand, impossible to see or touch with our eyes and hands. Humanity is now generating new life through synthetic biology by taking tools and machinery to the highest levels of sophistication. Computation, mathematics and linguistics is now generating the first "thinking entities" by exploiting elaborated models such as artificial neural networks that simulate the workings of neural cells. It is undoubtedly clear and "obvious" that humans think. Thinking is, in this way, a "familiar" and "obvious" phenomenon of our everyday lives and it is precisely why we will discuss it next as a matter. A subtle but intriguing idea might strike us at once as provoking. Put in the form of a question: is thinking what we mostly do with the mind? Why are thinking, reason and logics taking such a predominant place in our modern discussions on the mind and who we are? We start by pointing out that by claiming that we think alone we are not in a position to guarantee or clarify whether we can be said to be conscious or understand what others, including our "selves", say. That we think alone does no explain what thinking is or that we know what thinking is either even if we follow the mechanisms of thinking with the most powerful microscopes. Nevertheless, that thinking seems to naturally come to us as we live our everyday lives gives us a direction in the journey of the questioning of the mind and thinking. In this way, as we direct ourselves into a journey, we find ourselves already directed to a journey. This being already directed reminds us of Bohm when discussing the matter and "duality" of things and thoughts. It reminds us in that as we are about to discuss thinking and direct ourselves toward a path of "saying" we find ourselves already thinking and surrounded by a neighborhood of thought, even if we cannot clearly make out the exact path. This already being directed where we are already engaged with a "toward a path" - that we have encountered and that clears as we "lean toward" it - provides us with a sign in this chapter that we are to follow.

We start by claiming that since thinking seems to be so rooted and related to the concept of the mind and consciousness, we are legitimated to abuse these terms provided we always clarify what we mean. Our first statement regarding our "everyday" encounter with "consciousness" follows: consciousness is a game that is already and continuously "our" game. We continuously play this game through discussing it, embracing it or ignoring it. Consciousness "allows" us to "see" but we can also "ignore" the call of consciousness. In this way, it is not only that consciousness owns us. As consciousness calls for our attention, we also own it. Our task at hand is now to listen to the phenomena that we already know and own. In this way, provided we "listen" to the phenomena of consciousness and what it is telling us, ultimately, we are to "say" to consciousness what it "is", not the other way around. This is even if we only have an "average" knowledge and understanding of what consciousness is because, proximally and for the most part, the possibility of being conscious is ours. In summary, with the average knowledge that we have about the terms related to consciousness and with the experience of our everyday lives, we can confidently claim that we are already familiar with consciousness. Thus, from this point onwards we employ the term "mind" to explore the phenomena that emerge from what we otherwise term "mind" on average and in our everyday language and life.

## The coming to the mind

That thinking appears as an "obvious" and "familiar" term that we can otherwise not fully understand strikes us again as constitutive of the structure of the mind. In this sense, the mind and the "is" of the mind appear to us as something as familiar and common as it is "unattended" as a question. As the mind deals with thoughts we are to explore the "is" of a thought also by questioning it. In any case, thoughts do, always "proximally and for the most part", come to us. We can distinguish between 1) thoughts that become prevalent in that they become the object of thought and 2) the way in which thought, and the object of thought, becomes the object of thought.

Let us start with the first point by stating that it is at least shocking and intriguing that amongst all other, a given object of thought comes to be the one that we direct our minds to. Put in the form of a question: why does an object of thought become prevalent amongst all other? Humans dare and say what things are by directing their minds to them and declaring what things are. One might say "I can tell what this situation is about.", "I know what the problem is. I've realized how to proceed to solve it." or "This game is great.". In all these cases we "have something in mind" and we "say" the "what" of what we have and the "is" of the "what". Our mind can be directed and pointed toward all objects of thought, including the mind itself, and explore the neighborhood of that toward what it points at. In that way, things are known. In as far as they are the objects which are pointed at, things are. That is, it seems that as we say, things are. We might say "This house is beautiful", "I feel very good today" or "That is not the point here". This does not mean however that for us to "say" sounds need to be found travelling through the air and captured to then be processed. Our saying does not have anything to do with actual sounds. Humans might "say" more with a "look" than what can be written in many pages of a book. We all know that proximally and for the most part and we are not to ignore such phenomena. It is then not a mere matter of having the right transfer function to communicate with "exactitude" that which we mean to the one that listens. But rather, the one that "listens", has the capacity to "see" in what we say.

Things are also in as far as their essence is singled out in the direction that the mind points toward them. We might say "I just realized something regarding my friendship with you" so we point at our friendship in a "direction" that we "never saw before". Pointing with the mind at something in a direction involves 1) exclusion and delimiting as an object of thought is singled out amongst all other and 2) a delimiting in the way in which the mind points at thoughts in a given direction and a given orientation. Regarding an object of thought humans might say to each other "we are seeing different things" or "we are thinking about the same thing". Regarding a given thing and the orientation of the mind toward it we might say "you are seeing this from another point of view" or "we are looking at it differently". In that way, to the mind, everything and anything has the potential to become the object of thought as the mind points at it with a given orientation in a given direction.

It is otherwise also intriguing that objects of thought are always an object of thought to the mind while the mind is not an object of thought to other than the mind. The mind can point and orient itself toward all that is. The mind itself can become the object of thought to itself as it can direct its pointing toward itself, but nothing else, other than a mind, can point at it and think it. In a sense, who we are becomes the object of thought as we direct our minds toward our minds and we point at them. By looking at ourselves we say: "I am fine." or "I am happy I came." Even more strongly we might say: "I think I have found out what is wrong with me." or "I know who I am.". We might call this self-pointing of the mind "self-reflection" provided we understand this term as one to be circumvented by clarifying what it is as we explore it, that is, as the "positive" phenomena surrounding it emerge. We previously said such phenomena relates to the distances between our "selves" but we are now to deal with the "saying".

If we have the capacity to "listen" and be "conscious" however, how can we call each other "unconscious" many times and appear to ourselves as "unconscious" in many situations? As it points, the mind focuses onto an object of thought and it becomes aware of what the object of thought is in as far as it points at it in a direction by excluding all other thoughts and directions. Consciousness, in this way, relates as much to pointing as it does to exclusion. The use of the term consciousness here will be clarified in terms of pointing and exclusion in that "we are said to be conscious" in as far as we can point toward and object of thought 1) and delimit it or otherwise 2) acknowledging it to neglect it by excluding it as we point and direct our minds toward other. By delimiting our thought and enforcing the exclusion of any other we appear as unconscious to other. The capacity to "hold consciousness in" or otherwise "open it up" is in this sense at stake. Delimiting is in any case both shocking and intriguing. Why is it both shocking and intriguing? Amongst the vast reservoir of what is to be thought about and the whole and vastness of what is encompassable by thought, one properly thinks by directing the mind into that which is to be thought about amongst all other. As we direct our minds and orient ourselves toward thinking, thoughts become stronger and clearer as if clearing a path. If the clearing is powerful enough, the thought gathers and strengthens in a way that we are now "clear in our minds" as to what we are saying and thinking; we are then ready to speak. As we say, we direct our mind toward a thought in a way that a neighborhood of thoughts takes over our minds and these hold us. As these hold us, the pointing and clearing of the path becomes prevalent, we stand in a position to think, argue and invoke logics strongly with conviction and belief. We become strong in what we see and say, so we position ourselves in our saying and we are ready to argue and state. In such cases, we might say "we understand the situation, the logics of the situation and the angle to tackle it". Regarding what "is" in relation to persuasion, conviction and belief, we can read two translations of Parmenides on the way of truth. We already quoted this part in a translation that reads "persuasion" rather than "conviction" or "belief". In the translation of John Burnet:

> *"The first, namely, that it is, and that it is impossible for it not to be, Is the way of belief, for truth is its companion – Parmenides."*

The online Stanford Encyclopedia of Philosophy on Parmenides reads:

*"The one, that it is and that it is not not to be, is the path of conviction, for it attends upon true reality – Parmenides."*

That the thought comes and clears as if clearing a path toward thinking however still does not clarify how the object of thought came to be. Put in the form of a question: what is that thing that comes to us as that which we think about and point our mind toward by orienting it toward a given direction? This anything should, in any case, be singular in as far as it comes from the vastness of all thoughts that can be in any way that we can think of anything. Why is the thought that gathers singular? If the mind is that which allows us to understand anything, what that anything is, is at least intriguing in that it comes to us as an object of thought that is singled out amongst all other. We dare to say that we happen to see what is real as we see what is in what comes to us in our pointing and positioning as we "lean toward" it. In this way, the object of thought comes to be as we "lean toward" and as it, in return, comes to the front. As things come to the front in the mind, we are ready to explore them and understand them. Does consciousness then include the capacity to understand anything? As consciousness is in that what we point at with our minds comes to the front to be explored and be what "is", being conscious has as much to do with bringing to the front as with displacing to the back and concealing what "is not". This is precisely what we mean by exclusion. If any, consciousness is a losing of all except of that which comes to the front, yet, there is a coming to the front in consciousness. Some have written[31]:

*"Within an attenuated system of awareness, a mind might be aware of much more than is being contemplated in a focused extended consciousness."*

The above statement seems to say that what is in focused consciousness is less in that it is delimited in the extension of what it points at. Heraclitus discusses humans and emphasizes that they don't know. Yet not knowing to humans takes place in the condition of the unknown in as far as what is not known could, otherwise, be known. The sayings go:

> *"They are like dogs: for dogs also bark at what they do not know – Heraclitus."*

> *"They are donkeys: donkeys like chaff better than gold. – Heraclitus."*

Heidegger also wrote:

> *"They continually deal with beings everywhere. Yet Being remains concealed to them. If Being is to open itself up, it itself must have rank and maintain it. – Heidegger."*

If consciousness relegates most to concealment, most of what "is", in the sense of the sentences above, remains concealed even through consciousness and in fact precisely because of consciousness. Consciousness however also deals with the known as what comes to the front. We said that there is something intriguing about the mind pointing at what comes to the front. Put as a question: what is to be known or revealed through consciousness? We are not intrigued here regarding the mechanisms or sensorial functions of the brain. The questioning does not concern whether and object of thought becomes the object of thought by free will, because it is the one selected as "logical", the one representing "reality itself", molecular mechanisms or other. We are not interested in saying as if asking whether we "seek" to say the "truth" or otherwise "deceive". Instead, our questioning concerns the imposing of the direction of the mind toward what it points at as well as how what it points at came to be what is pointed at. Our pointing puts thoughts in the condition of standing and holding up above all other as if by rank. In that pointing, our attention extends and leans toward exploring the unthought by opening and allowing some thoughts to prevail. The unthought is about to be but is not in that it remains concealed. The unthought is that which is not in that it stays concealed by our lack of pointing as we bring to the front what is to be thought. The experience of pointing with our minds, as humans, toward a thought, becomes in this way a breaking of all boundaries in that all that could be is displaced by our pointing and a thought becomes clear and singled out. We might say that we are then focused on a given matter. Humans say: "This job requires my exclusive attention. It requires that I stay focused." or "I can't afford any distraction. I need to pay attention to this matter only.". We might otherwise say: "I can't concentrate or focus since I'm too dispersed and I can't properly think." or "Everything calls my attention, so I can't focus or think.". There is indeed rank in the pointing of the mind. There is rank in consciousness and thinking. A rank however does not imply that something is primordial in that something is necessarily "superior" or "logically" ranked as that which should prevail above other because of "some supreme law" outside the listening or leaning toward what calls for our attention. The ranking takes place as the mind directs and holds onto that which comes as the matter of thought as a call. As we hold and maintain it, the thought prevails above other and we find ourselves "speaking our thoughts" by placing them to the front. That the call can be categorized "as that which corresponds" to a "real" and "valid" ranking corresponding to a "reality" outside the call, that is, to a "true" ranking that is above all, is not what concerns this ranking. Such terms are, if any, metaphysically obscure and act as veils to phenomena. In this way, correspondence with reality as there being a "true" reality is not our concern as such concern distracts us from the phenomena of the mind. The concern of the ranking is in that the ranking takes place as the call places the direction and sets us on track onto "something" rather than something else. That is, as it displaces other by clearing our "path" to a thought. In the phenomena of the mind, there is a thought to the front. Our discussion so far even implies that consciousness, awareness and attention require that we are "oblivious" to anything other than what is present and to the front. Thus, consciousness ranks in order and reveals what "is" by attending it while excluding all other. The other appears as absent and unattended. We summarize the first point with another question: why would an object of thought come to be amongst all other, concealing all other, and why is there an orientation of the mind toward it?

*Sergio Santos, Matteo Chiesa and Maritsa Kissamitaki.*

## The seeking of the mind

We start with a question: how can a thought prevail above all other and reign above all to then allow any other come to the front? It is also our concern how a thought "comes to the front" when we presumably, and sometimes, had "nothing" to the front. These questions concern the singling out of thoughts, that is, the directing and orienting of our minds so that thoughts can become the object of thought to then fall, as they came themselves from the fallen, or redirect, as we are to think other. We can summarize our discussion so far as follows: humans think by directing their minds in a way that what they point toward, and their pointing toward by orienting themselves to a thought, matter. That is, the object of thought and orientation toward the thought, but also the direction that we point at with our minds, matter. The directionality of the mind "speaks" to us as if "seeking" a "toward" in the form of a "direction". But why would we point and direct our mind toward a matter of thought in the first place? The answer to this question is clear when we look at it superficially and we do not try to bring the question forth in a way that it reaches its full extension and reach. With this question we are seeking the "what" of our minds in as far as we are humans. That is, we are not talking – only, and it is also not our main question here - about the everyday things that happen to us where we use our mind to orient ourselves "correctly" in our "toward". For example, we are not talking about "needing" to know how to predict the weather if we are thinking about going to the beach tomorrow and that, "of course", there is a clear direction in the methodology of predicting the weather. If any, this would be a theme for predictive AI which is already accomplishing its task successfully and for a reason. Namely, the field is well founded as it follows the correct direction to its aim. What is then the relationship between understanding, mind and the orientation of the mind toward a matter of thought in the sense that we are humans? Why do we seek orientation and direction? When we can tell that others don't understand what we "see", we call their attention, so they can "see" what we "see". That is, when people say that in their saying there is something to be said in a way that it gives meaning to their saying as far as the mind is oriented toward what it points at, they are calling for a reorientation of the mind. This reorientation presumably points at that which "is" in a way that it can be understood. Their call appears in the form of a "persuasion" or "suggestion" to our mind.

Predictive AI, on the other hand, might reason by providing arguments that are stronger than what any person might provide. A question that we could ask AI today would then be: is there something that "is"? Is the task of AI to find that which "is"? If the "sayings" pointing at what "is" are pointing at what is real while all other sayings are not, isn't what is logical a single necessary path and the single object of real thought? Is this not "seeking" the "seeking" for a "universal" that can be turned into a "relative" truth at any time? That is, are we to "look for" "universals" making this our main task - in the way of, and - following "Platonic", "Aristotelian" and "Medieval" ontology? That the concept of "universals" is not "driving" our "seeking" is, in any case, obscure and definitely not clear. That we are "seeking" the "truth" as "universals" can be traced to such ancient ontologies even in our modern laws[32]. That some "seeking" appear as "genuine" must then relate to a conforming of the mind toward that which already "orients" our minds today through metaphysics. Whether a historical revision of what "is" is in place is to be seen and not to be ignored by current research in AI. That we continuously "deal" with metaphysics, even as we ignore them, does not, in this way, guarantee that what is to be "sought" is "simply obvious". Listening to any current street talk, friendly talk or other everyday talk, the emergence of the "universal" is otherwise "obvious" and stubbornly appears. Returning to AI: Do strong and robust arguments seem to call to a single path in terms of what truly "is"? What is the place of "reorienting" for such entities? How are we all, as humans, to reorient and conform with that which we are told "is"? Again, this question does not concern the actual ability to find what is, as opposed to what is not, and what should be the object of thought as opposed to what it should not be. The question concerns the existence of such thoughts as the ones that are, how they come to be and whether we are to conform as humans. The question relates to the existence of uniqueness in as far as what is as opposed to what it is not. The question relates to conforming. That is, if our path is to find what "is" and what "is" is to guide us, the only path left seems to be to conform. Some might term what "is" simply "truth". Such sayings are far from unintriguing however. For example, if there is "truth", what is it? Why do we have to conform? Also, regarding its essence: Why does "truth" appear as the object of thought and why is it to be reasoned so it can be? The "...so it can be" is key in our last question and in what Parmenides says of thought and being. Parmenides said:

*"... in fact it is the same to think and to be. - Parmenides"*

A thought can be the object of thought to the mind in as far as the mind directs itself toward it so it points at it. In other words, in as far as it comes to the front we think what "is", that is, we "see" what "is". So why would anything need to be logical and reasonable before it is brought to the front? How can logics simply unfold without a mind that points? Put in the form of a formal question: is what is logical and reasonable, that is, strong arguments that are self-evident and valid, the whole of what truly is? As we deal continuously with logics and reason where language is organized, and arguments ordered and logically structured, we could say that the strength of the argument and the lack of internal contradiction stands for valid thoughts and thinking. Everything else is not what appears to be. Logics are sometimes said to point at the thoughts that truly are as these are "correct". Even in our saying "we should be illogical sometimes", logics and truth still resonate in our saying. Here we are concerned with the terms "logics", "logic" and "logical" as these appear in our everyday lives as we face "real" decisions that concern us. That is, as truth and logics come to the front as what "truly" guides us in our lives. With this we clarify that standard logic, such as propositional, mathematical or other forms of technical logic, are not taken here as our theme. In our everyday lives we might "seek" logics even by sometimes claiming to ignore them as we say: "That's not logical.", "Why are you behaving so illogically?" or "Life is not about logics.". That is, even in that sometimes we claim to ignore logics, logics still appear as a reference to us. In this way, some thoughts and arguments are valid, whereas others are not. In our saying we point toward what "is". Yet a human might say or understand more with a look than what can be written into a book. Whether a "look" has "logics" to be found is what is at stake in terms of the phenomena of the mind in our being human. For a human to say to another, the one that listens needs to point at the object of thought in the direction and with the orientation that thought is to be oriented. For us to be directed and oriented we do not even need "sound" or "hearing". We might just "look" at someone and "know". This last sentence can act as our guide to understand "consciousness" provided we pay attention to the phenomena that emerge in "seeing", "listening" and "understanding" phenomenologically.

Logics and reasoning deal with the essence of contradiction. It is said that provided there are no contradictions things "are". Most arguments "attack" contradiction even in our everyday lives irrespective of what we mean by "contradiction" and even if the term "contradiction" is ignored as a question. In the philosophy of Hegel however, even contradictions are "logically" surmounted through "logic". The logic of Hegel is not a logic of mathematics or a form of logic that we might have seen in technical studies, mathematics, engineering or physics. If any, the logic of Hegel deals with metaphysics and what "is". Such "logic" is relatively modern, approximately 200 years old, and will allow us to see where ancient Greece reveals the "is" of our modern thinking as it fundamentally differs from it. We now turn to Hegel's writings regarding "Dialectics" or "the method of the contradictory process between opposing sides"[33]:

> *"According to the logic of a traditional* reductio ad absurdum *argument, if the premises of an argument lead to a contradiction, we must conclude that the premises are false—which leaves us with no premises or with nothing – on Hegel."*

We see that premises might lead us through logics to contradiction as we argue and provide arguments. Once we fall into contradictions, what is it that is left?

> *"We must then wait around for new premises to spring up arbitrarily from somewhere else, and then see whether those new premises put us back into nothingness or emptiness once again, if they, too, lead to a contradiction. Because Hegel believed that reason necessarily generates contradictions,*

*Sergio Santos, Matteo Chiesa and Maritsa Kissamitaki.*

*he thought new premises will indeed produce further contradictions. – on Hegel"*

What is left is "a waiting around"*. Stating that this waiting around will lead to an arbitrary premise that springs up from somewhere is on the other hand deficient to us. Deficient in that it does not clarify any working of the mind in terms of what we seek here, namely, describing the condition of humans and the phenomena of the mind. If we just say we "are" to wait around, we are not clarifying what this "waiting around" is phenomenologically. This waiting around is just there in front of us as something that "happens" or is just "said" but is otherwise nothing to the mind. It appears or sounds like a mechanistic mind that is simply "paused" or "stuck". A formal question can then be placed as follows: what "is" this waiting around for something to come to the mind? This question might give us to think. The question appears as thought-provoking in that it seems to "hide" something that we are "familiar" with but is otherwise relegated to the "oblivion" as a question. If we are to understand "waiting around" phenomenologically we are to do so from what we find in our everyday lives as a "waiting around". This is the direction that will orient our seeking.

In all respects, waiting around for a thought sounds familiar and it is something that we already "know" in some way and otherwise fully. We find ourselves "waiting around" in our everyday lives in that sometimes nothing comes to our minds. Eventually, the mind points at an object of thought and we can "see", "say" and "speak" of things or for a matter. Throughout our lives and in our everyday lives we see and say. We talk about what "is" with others as we also listen to others speak about what "is". Sometimes we "see" what "is" and other times we don't "see" it. This also happens to others that talk to us. In between "seeing", "saying" and "listening" we sometimes "see" nothing. Hegel speaks of "nothingness"

---

* We are here abusing the term "wait around" that might rather be used to contrast Hegel to Plato. Nevertheless, the concept could very well speak of Hegel's readings on the philisophy of Plato. The reader can refer to any text on Hegel's dialectics or the online database https://plato.stanford.edu under the Hegel's dialectics entry, from where some of the quotes have been taken in this work.

as emerging in our "wait around" for "something". Hegel also says that before seeing nothing, and as we find ourselves "seeing" and providing arguments, we are led by premises. It is only "eventually", and as we are led, presumably by logics, that we encounter such "nothingness" through contradiction. Again, presumably, contradiction comes after a path that ends up as a "waiting around". Reading any dialogue of Plato might help us understand what Hegel means with this "being put back into nothingness" as we "encounter contradiction". We could read any of the dialogues of Socrates by Plato for example. Yet, we claim that it is not clear whether such seeing nothing "hides" something or it is "simply nothing". We anticipate that a very different "waiting around" emerges as a possibility to the human mind. That is, a condition of the mind emerges as "disoriented" or "fallen" rather than as a condition of "doubt" or "waiting around" for an idea or solution to a problem. For now, however, our concern is the "logics" that are told to us, or that we tell ourselves, in as far as they might reveal "something" about what the mind "is".

Many times, we find ourselves telling each other: "Don't you see the logics of our procedure?", "It's very logical that we proceed in this way." or "I don't see the logics in what you say." That logics are "true" in that they relate to the essence of "truth", are or are not contradictory or even whether they are "well established as a method" to argue or communicate, does not say much to us regarding the phenomena of the mind in our everyday lives. If any, "logics" many times appear to us as a "saying" that is "just repeated" but otherwise does not concern us. The sciences and current machine learning and AI typically see logics and define them for their ability to "direct" us or algorithms in the aiming at a target. As logics work their way they give us the solution that we seek. It is therefore very clear why we would hold logics as our companion in the day. We decidedly use logics everyday to accomplish most of the tasks of our everyday lives as they present themselves throughout the day. Other times "logics" appear as a weapon to confront others, as a form of "tyranny" thrown onto us or as something that we simply do not "understand" or care about. It is possible to treat logics in a way that we are "indifferent" to what "logics" have to say in what they say, because to us, they might "say" nothing. For many people, the whole concept of the logic of Hegel might say "nothing". So, these people might encounter such "nothingness", that maybe Hegel is talking about, as soon as they read about the Dialectics of Hegel. These people do not even "follow" the logic of Hegel when they read the sentences because the logic in the sentences is just "a sentence" or a "set of sentences". In this way, even if we are not thinking the logic of Hegel and following any of his arguments, we might think that they are "nothing". Yet, we might still claim that "logics" are to guide us and we invoke logics in our everyday lives. This alone gives us to think and might signal a path in our discussion.

Let us now provide a statement regarding truth, logics, predictive AI and contradiction: "the truth and logics that concern sayings that are "logical" and deduced from "logics", are not, and cannot be, fundamental in the foundation of what comes to be and, therefore, in the question of what being is, let alone the structure of the mind and consciousness." Truth and logics follow only when we are already pointing at what conforms. That is, we can think only as we already conform with what "is". The pointing and direction of the mind are what is at stake and, in any case, precede thinking in that they point or open a path toward thought, i.e. to conform to logics one must "lean toward" that which such logics point and into the direction and orientation that such logics point. Hegel might have termed such leaning toward "the movement of the spirit" – even though we clarify that Hegel's Dialectics are not what we seek here as constitutive of the structure of the mind. Hegel's dialectics remain an "outsider" to the constitutive phenomena of the mind. Whether such logics are correct, contradictory or simply words emerge as phenomena of the mind only as a possible "engagement" of the mind with that which can be "understood", "used", "ignored", "dreaded" or other in them. We might even say about the logic of Hegel that "it doesn't make sense" and move on to "our lives" and our "logics". Logics are therefore not "truth" or a "guide" that speaks of, or structures, the workings of the mind constitutively. Let alone they can produce an argument that we "must" follow. But rather, logics appear in our everyday lives as what we must embrace, ignore, follow or confront in its sayings, in our "living alongside others" or as opposing or agreeing with our "true deep self" or other "selves". That is, regarding what we face in our everyday lives, Hegel's dialectics are "alien" to what "is" phenomenologically. For this reason, Hegel's dialectics are concerning to the "mind" in a similar way that modern logic, calculus or arithmetic might concern us. Technical logics appear in our everyday lives as a "tool" to an end that is to be "understood" to such end. To understand the subtlety of the phenomena that the "waiting around" might be "hiding" from us, we must face it in our everyday lives as such waiting emerges. First phenomena to have emerged in our discussion already relates to the character of the "logics" of what "is" as something alien to "logics" itself. This last sentence appears as strange and it should not be misunderstood. What we say here has nothing to do with "sounding illogical" or, as in informal logic or natural language[34], the saying that "informal logic is not logic at all". "Logics" are somehow alien to our everyday lives but otherwise "always" present. They are always present in that they appear as familiar but otherwise alien in that they also appear as "ambiguously" unclear as to their relation to us. This "ambiguity" emerges in the life of even the most skillful mathematician no matter how consistent his technical logic might be. If one claims that the logic of Hegel, Plato's dialogues or other types of "logic", are not present in our everyday lives, one only needs to "listen" and "attend" to their everyday lives for a while, as if "waiting around" for a while. As we "listen" and "attend" to our everyday lives we will experience the uprooting and abrupt manifestation of such "logics" as a "happening". This is the violent placing of "logics" that is "unique to humans". We will explore this condition in greater detail below. For now, we quote a saying of Heidegger regarding what humans are. The description of terms is left to the next pages. Heidegger wrote:

> *"Humans are* δεινόν *twice, in a way that is unique to humans, that is,* το δεινότατον. *Humans exert violence and are the most violent: violence-doing in the midst of the overwhelming violence. – Heidegger."*

We now concern ourselves with "disorientation" rather than "orientation". If the mind can be "oriented" or has the capacity to "orient" itself "toward" anything, it is because of its inherent orientability. In as far as orientability is inherent to the mind, the mind also comes with the possibility to lack orientation or for the orientation to appear as if "swaying". As we are oriented we might also, and at any point, just collapse. That is, the orientation and even the orientability of the mind might "collapse" fully and the mind is then "at a loss" and deficient in its capacity to "work". As the mind has an inherent orientability it also has an inherent directionality, that is, the mind actively "seeks" for orientation in as far as a "toward" that involves a "need", an "in order to" or a "for what".

In any case, a "real" collapse of the mind in our everyday lives has nothing to do with the "contradictions" of the logics of Hegel or modern logics that make us "wait around". That is, this "waiting around" has nothing to do with the "abyss" that Nietzsche referred to above or what we discussed regarding the "abyss" of what is and what "is not" of Parmenides. If any, the "waiting around" of Hegel, academic logic or everyday life doubt and use of logics, appears as an academic "abyss" instead. With everyday doubt here, we refer to such doubts that come about when we are "doubting" or "lost" as to how to come up with a good idea or with a solution to a given problem. This everyday "waiting around" however, does appear as phenomena of the mind in as far as we are trying to decide or think because we have lost site of a "direction" in our mind, or because we have lost track of an argument. While this "weak" waiting around of our everyday lives has already been discussed above, it is worth exploring it again in order to contrast it with the "abyss" that Nietzsche was talking about. We write the quote again here to remind us of the "dreadful" abyss:

> *"Beware that, when fighting monsters, you yourself do not become a monster... for when you gaze long into the abyss. The abyss gazes also into you. – Nietzsche."*

Nietzsche speaks of monsters. This is really a very different "abyss" when comparing it to a "waiting around" altogether even if one invokes nothingness, emptiness or collapse of logics. Let us start by claiming that even if the "waiting around" is "truly" serious academically or intellectually, in that we do not find a way to avoid logical contradiction or other, such waiting might present us with an intellectual "abyss", but it is not the theme that we are seeking here. That is, waiting around might appear in our everyday lives as a "concerning ambiguity" or "concerning emptiness" that otherwise does not appear as a "real concern" to our "task at hand" in our everyday lives, i.e. the mind does not "fully collapse". This is irrespective of how much we might like or engage ourselves with our work or "task at hand". It is not a matter of enthusiasm or care either. Even as we are enthusiastic or care about our tasks we already conform with them. We might suffer at work or with our hobby and we might experience "chaos", but this is still not the "abyss" that we seek. In fact, we might conform even more genuinely with what we do the more we care about it even if "it doesn't make any sense". If we understand conforming with "having our minds busy with something", that we don't find an answer or solution to something does not mean that we have "lost our mind". That is, in as far as we are "already looking or waiting" we have not "collapsed". The collapse that concerns us as constitutive of the phenomena of the mind, emerges as the mind itself seems to collapse in as far as it loses track of any "toward" and "need". The collapse of the mind does not involve a "not finding a solution" only. But rather, it involves the incapacity to orient itself toward a "toward" that holds us as "who we are". In this losing we face the loss of "having lost our mind". That is, the collapse that we seek here refers to the inherent orientability and directionality of the mind being at stake. We might say: "She lost her mind.", or "He doesn't know what to do with himself. He's truly lost." The saying of these sentences does not fully explain what we "know" to be at stake when we "lose our minds". That we cannot even explain such collapse with words tells us that there is something very "familiar" about it. We do not seem to "understand" fully what it is but we otherwise "know" it very well. The collapse that we refer to is such that "truly losing the mind" is appreciated by even "seeing" the "losing oneself" in someone's eyes, face or expression. An expression could then "tell" us all and "speak" for itself. The more disoriented the mind, the more "dreadful" the phenomena of "disorientation" appears. In this way, the mind deals with disorientation or the condition of the fallen as a constitutive part of what the mind is. Collapse also appears as if by rank, that is, the "losing oneself" appears by rank in the sense that there is hierarchy in losing the mind. A question now emerges that can direct our thought? How does the "losing our mind" relate to the "abyss" and "monsters" of Nietzsche? This is a question that will be clarified in terms of what it "says" in the next lines. In any case, the "abyss" of the monsters of Nietzsche always presents itself as a menace to humans, but also as a well of wealth. Nietzsche wrote:

> *"Verily, I had to fly to the highest spheres that I might find the fount of pleasure again. Oh, I found it, my brothers! Here, in the highest spheres, the fount of pleasure wells up for me. – Nietzsche."*

The possibility to experience such "terrible", but also possibly "blissful", sight emerges as familiar and prevalent in all "seeing" or "not seeing" but also in the "losing our minds altogether" to then maybe "see". We sometimes say: "I can't seem to see things as clearly as I saw them yesterday.", "I lost track of what I was talking about.", or "Give me some time to see if I get inspired again and I get a better grasp of this issue." More strongly we might say: "I feel like everything around me is collapsing. My whole world is collapsing", "I lost my purpose in life altogether." or "A new reality appeared in front of me. I am a new person." Hegel refers to the condition of fallen or disoriented somehow mysteriously with the term "waiting around" but the "waiting around" remains alien to the fallen mind that we are discussing here. It is at this point worth considering what might be said in self-help or motivational books. Self-help books are precisely a place where humans that find themselves disoriented or even experience "full mental collapse" might look for direction or orientation. Such losing orientation in these self-help, motivational[35] or inspirational[36] books emerges as something somehow much closer to us as humans than the "waiting around" of Hegel. Some examples of what self-help books might say follow:

> *"If you do not decide what you want and who you want to be, others will decide it for you."*

> *"Think positive thoughts."*

> *"While many people consider sensory experience as the main source of happiness, really it is peace of mind. What destroys peace of mind is anger, hatred, anxiety and fear. Kindness*

*counters this—and through appropriate education we can learn to tackle such emotions. - Dalai Lama, 2018-July"*

The above sayings talk about deciding, that is, directing our mind and orienting it. They also talk about objects of thought that come as the object of thought that will orient us. There is always that which must come to the front as what is in the "saying". Even the orientation of the mind toward what comes is given. In other words, there is no time "to wait around" or "fall", there is only a "need", i.e. to "take" what comes at hand and delivered. The object of thought in these sayings is always present in that there is no signal and no call to the mind other than "taking" what "is". While Hegel talks of opposing sides, these sayings come as a clear side, delimited, directed and sharp in their direction, even as they also talk about an opposite direction sometimes. The waiting around does not come as a "pleasant" waiting, nor even as a "disturbing" waiting. There is simply "no waiting" and the saying presents itself as a "sentence". We are to be very subtle in our search for the emerging phenomena of the mind when we consider these sayings and their relationship to "logics", "waiting around" and the "abyss" of Nietzsche. It is somehow strange that there is even something "uncanny" about such sayings. They are "obviously" directing us in the right direction as it appears as very "logical". What comes out of the "well" is already given as it has already been found. That is, the logical direction has been found. We must emphasize again that the sayings above are not even considered here in terms of whether they are good, bad or correct. However, less formally we understand that they are almost certainly directing us into that which is "good", "correct" and "logical" for the most part. If this is so, why are we talking about them and questioning them? The emergency is in conforming with them and following their directiveness. On the other hand, why is something about them emerging as familiar, ambiguous and subtle? We claim that such sayings even appear as "uncanny" somehow.

Since the sentences strike us as somehow "unattackable" and "final", in that they are most certainly correct, but still there is a sense of familiarity, ambiguity and uncanniness about them, we might start by questioning when one might attack the sentences in "real" life. We clarify that we are not talking here about "going against" such thing as "happiness" in our intellectual lives or discussions. That would be the "real" of Hegel's logic if any. We are talking about our everyday lives as these are "at stake". Sometimes we say: "Don't you dare to philosophize in situations like this.", "The last thing we need now is some random quote." or, more strongly and informally, "That is just bullshit" or "My life is hell! Shut up!". Even though when we attack sentences that typically appear in motivational or self-help books we are likely facing very "serious" problems and are likely not "seeing things clearly", such "attacks" still seem to say something. That is, we might "strongly attack" such sayings precisely when "we lose our minds". So far what strikes us the most is the uncanniness and the correctness of the sentences that are otherwise sometimes "attacked" when we "lose our minds". The deconstruction of our thoughts seems to follow in this way:

Motivational sayings might appear as uncanny even when they are right and as we try to comply. The uncanniness appears subtly as such sayings appear as "already" familiar in terms of the "correctness" of what they say. There is otherwise the "semblance" of "depth" in that they present themselves as "unattackable" and "meaningful" to us but still as "just a sentence". The sayings appear with an object, a clear direction and a clear reject of the opposite. That these sayings point at the "need" for us to be "directed", or at the necessity to direct ourselves toward something, seems also "correct". The minds "seeks" to be directed as we live our lives. We are then to explore these sayings with the hope that the phenomena of the mind emerge to the surface from the most "obvious" everyday experiences. In this way, we might clarify the essence of the "uncanniness" and "unattackability" that manifests in the sayings. We start then by exploring the phenomena that emerged at once, even if ambiguously and proximally and for the most part, as soon as we read the sentences above.

The objects of thought are delivered at hand to orient us as they speak to us to "persuade" us. In as far as they are seeking to persuade us they speak for a matter that is to make us think in a very delimited way. Delimited in that their being delivered at hand negate the possibility of any enquiry as to either object or direction. That is, they come already directed to what "is" and in the direction that "should be". What this is "is", or how it came to be, is relegated to either other things that follow them or to the ambiguity and violence of stating as "oblivion". This ambiguity and violence come as the uprooting of these sayings. In this way, for example, when we are said to consider "peace of mind" we might be given a negative direction such as "anger" and a positive direction such as "kindness". One can only take a direction as one "already conforms". We further seem to somehow always and already conform even when at times we might fight the direction or reject it when we "truly fall" and "lose our minds". The "losing our minds" is then the sign to be read.

The answer to the uncanniness might strike us at once as we refer to "losing our minds". This is because the "sayings" of the sentences cannot reach where they lose site of their grounding. When one shakes the grounding of the "sayings" one dares to "live outside their limits". This is so in these sayings and in any legitimate field of science no matter how well grounded or how successfully it uproots toward its targets. The sayings of these books uproot toward a "toward" that cannot answer nor ground the "uprooting" of the sayings. The grounding of their uprooting might thus give us the answer. Where do these sayings lead us? What is that which they want to leave behind by directing themselves "toward" their path? What was their call? Their call is always founded in "getting out of the abyss" and not "even looking at it" as one risks "losing the mind". That is, as one risks "losing oneself" as monsters meet us. Their call is to "flee" in the opposite direction at all costs. That we now have the answer to their grounding and call might not clarify the meaning of the call. We have to "hear" the call to "understand" it. Thus, as we found the answer we might have "read" it but missed the "saying" in it. The "thought-provoking" in its saying might then appear as a "saying" or a word. Since the sentences here refer to the two previous chapters of the book we will break them down in the lines below. In the next lines we will also "bring forth" what the "saying" of our "answer" has to "say".

Let us start by arguing that one might follow a "path down" in decomposing concepts or ideas. Thus, we can proceed to go down the path of decomposing the sayings. In this way, if "peace of mind" is what we seek, the path down takes us to "happiness" as what grounds "peace of mind". Whether there is another step on this "path down toward other foundations" is typically left unsaid in a way that "happiness" appears as an uprooting ground. The uprooting of the ground manifests itself always as the "abyss" that can otherwise "shake" at any moment. The shaking is only protected in that its questioning is somehow "ignored". We must also emphasize that in many of these statements there is no direct fundamental call even though the sentences might claim that we need to orient ourselves, decide and point. That they call to point, while the direction is already given, implies that the pointing already happened, that is, we were not involved in the pointing. Said in other words, we were not involved in the making of the "who we are" in as far as who we "are" to "be" is many times the target of such sayings. Such sayings many times target who we are in our everyday lives whether in the company of ourselves only or in the company of others. We could interpret these sentences as a call that took place to the absent present. We are absent in the call and present at having it delivered at hand. We are also present in that we are "there in front of ourselves and others", but absent in that, even if we heard the call that directed these sayings, we might not have "heard" it. The call otherwise appears in this sense as a mystery to us. Since we did not "hear" nor "answer" the call of these sayings, both their grounding and their direction mysteriously appear to us as a sentence at hand. It is "of course" the path. The most striking is that the "leaning toward" takes place even if we did not "hear" a call. We are otherwise "told" to lean and "conform".

We would now like to clarify that our intention is not to work against the sayings of self-help or motivational books. Our questioning has nothing to do with them since their direction is alien to the theme of our questioning the mind. As in the case of predictive AI and current views on "truth" and "logics", arguments and logics come already in the direction and orientation that is given and they are not to be "opposed". As in predictive AI and sciences in general, the methods followed are not to be questioned here. What these sayings offer is always a direction that is to be followed to the "end" that they are made to serve. We can even confidently claim that they mostly serve their purpose well. Having clarified what is not our intention we can now proceed with our task. The question still is: why do these sayings appear as correct, unattackable and yet attackable when one "loses the mind"? The sense of uncanniness can also guide our next discussion. Why do these sayings appear as uncanny even when we know them to be guiding us to what we know to be correct?

What self-help and motivational books are telling us relates to finding arguments and logics. The logics however are to always be guided "toward" what is already given, that is, their end. Their end further strikes us as what comes immediately in them as a sentence at hand. Their end is as obvious and clear as unambiguous, yet uncanny. Many popular sayings might go: "pursue happiness", "what matters is peace of mind", "positive thoughts are to be your guide" or "focus on positive thoughts". What many saying have in common is that they already provide an object of thought, a direction and an orientation as if what is to be avoided, always, is to "not have any". This avoiding to "not be oriented" at all costs emerges in this way as something. Finally, this is the emerging phenomena of the mind that we were seeking. What emerges as "something" is the "fear" to "lose our mind". That is, the direction of our mind and the inherent orientability and directionality of the mind is to be protected at all costs. If we "don't have a direction" we "lose site" of all and "lose our own mind". The directionality and orientability of the mind itself, that is the structure of the mind is at stake. That is, what is to be protected at all cost is "the mind itself". For what is the worst fear, the worst terror of a human if not "losing the mind"? Is not this not contemplating the possibility of not having a direction, and even a call to avoiding not having something to "guide" us and "direct" us, a positive emerging phenomenon in these sentences? This "fear" to not be able to "hear", nor "say", nor "point" with our minds, that is, the fear to appear fully unconscious to all, secures these sayings in their grounding and is "not to be looked at again in the face". In this way, the "fear" of not having a direction emerges as the genuine call that grounded the sentences themselves. This grounding is our "abyss". Only when we fall into the "abyss" and we "lose our mind completely" we would "dare" to face the kind of monster that would lead us to even question the validity of these saying. The ungrounded ground that "grounded" these books, that is, the uprooting in most of these sayings, emerges as an intention to "avoid" not having a direction at all cost. This fear does not emerge as a "waiting around" that simply confuses us or where we struggle to find a solution. It looks like these sayings are rooted in the uprooting grounds of the constitutive structure of the mind itself. We might put the question as follows again: why are we to avoid "not having any direction" and why is "not having a direction" not even considered as a question and even dreaded as a question? Having "no positive direction" would be attacking the very structure of the mind itself. In as far as the sayings of motivational and self-help books protect the structure of the mind, attacking them is attacking the mind itself. What is at stake in such attacks is the structure of our minds. This might explain the "uncanniness" that we might feel at even suggesting attacking these sayings. As we hear, we "know" that we are to comply as we can just take their message. When we "feel" that the motivational quote or self-help book is directing us in the direction that "protects" our mind, we "know" the books are telling us the "truth". This is how "true" motivational quotes and "true" and "meaningful" self-help books appear as "logically" telling us the "truth".

There is still one subtle detail that, ambiguous and familiar as it might sound or feel, might also result in some sense of "uneasiness" or "uncanniness". That is, motivational and self-help books always "point" into a direction, but this does not mean to point at any direction at random at all. We say that these books warn us above all to "never fall", that is, to "never lose our mind". Still, there is always directionality in them. In other words, if any, they talk about opposite directions and they mostly tell us that one, i.e. the opposite, is a place to never go. Such opposite directions or dualisms typically relate to "good" and "evil", "health" or "illness", "happiness" or "unhappiness". These opposites do not appear as a "mere choice" as if we could one day decide to move into one direction and the next to the other and it would be the same "altogether". The opposite direction - to be contrasted to the opposing sides of Hegel - always appears as the "most dreadful", "uncanny" and "unknown". There is a no land that is never to be our home. If we ever find ourselves just "waiting around" for thought, they recommend and warn "to never take the opposite direction". They recommend it in such a subtle way that it is not even recommended explicitly. It is already presented as so dreadful that it is "obviously" wrong to even question it. That these sayings are still metaphysical in that they rely on "un1questioned" words that are "placed" in front of us is not our concern now. Our concern now is their target as their "toward", including the experiencing of the "waiting around" in these sayings. These are very different again to the "waiting around" of Hegel. This difference takes us closer to the abrupt speeches of the ancient Greeks and far from the academic, peaceful talk of Hegel. Even further from the alien "sayings" of "formal" logic and linguistics. When one is to be "logical" there is a single path. The saying of the Dalai lama above is particularly interesting in this respect. The saying talks about the opposites as "hatred", "anxiety", "anger" and "fear". But it does not talk about a possibility. That is, the opposite is not a direction "to be sought" for the mind. If any, it is to be "escaped", "feared" and "dreaded". This dread shows us that the genuine foundation of motivational books has nothing to do with enthusiasm in the sense of a comfortable or peaceful happiness. The uprooting of these quotes, sayings and methods for the mind, ground themselves in protecting the structure of the mind as the "who" of "who we are". Thus, the grounding of motivational books rests, always, in providing an orientation as an alternative to the "falling" so to avoid the most dreaded of all, namely, losing it all as one simply "loses the mind". How does this have to do with opposites? If we take the opposite, we are warned – implicitly and many times without saying it - that we will "simply lose our mind". Is it coincidental that we use the expression "have you lost your mind", "what the hell is wrong with you?" or "are you insane?" when we "oppose" what we consider to be "sacred" directions or paths? In their potential to "see", "experience" or "walk into" the opposite sides, humans appear as δεινόν. In that "any" thought might come to the front in a clear direction to us humans, we are δεινόν. This explains why we are δεινόν twice. We are δεινόν in that we can experience the "losing our own minds" according to others but also experience the "losing the minds of others", including the world itself, as they, or the world, confront us. As the direction of humans appears as δεινόν, any direction appears as "the most violent placing". We discuss δεινόν further in the lines below. Suffice it to say that we use the Greek term because what it means is explained not only as a word, but as an explanation to be explored.

The above finding could be said to be the most thought-provoking in that it strikes us as what is to be thought about most dreadfully. The thought of it makes us shake. That is, the protection of the very structure of our mind is not to be questioned. Working against our own mind is the path to true collapse. This "fear" of "losing our mind" is so familiar and stubborn in our everyday lives, but otherwise so ambiguous and strange, that only now we see the "uncanniness" in the sayings. The uncanniness emerges from the grounding of the sayings in that such ungrounded grounds uproot, and they are not to be touched. Their uprooting is not to be questioned. Even if our worst enemy tells us to guide our lives with "happiness" we are to "comply" and never question it. One only needs to attempt to work against the sayings of motivational and self-help books to understand "fear", "terror" and "dread". On the other hand, it is by having the capacity to "look" that we are "humans" and have a "human mind".

In summary, the mind seeks to be directed and the falling is to be "feared". Through its inherent directionality and orientability the mind "seeks" a direction that will "protect" the mind. Fear appears as a "losing our minds". The mind is then guided primordially by the need of not "falling" as it "fears" the fall even when "falling" might not even be considered as a possibility. As the mind is directed the mind understands. The mind is thus guided and stays high up in its direction toward the "known" as its target and path. High up there the mind "sees" and "questions" but is always confronted and facing the possibility to "fall". This "falling" might come with any shaking. Any shaking or "sway" is then also to be avoided in as far as we "fear" the fall and we "seek" to understand. In this way we "seek" refuge in "wise" sayings that direct us into friendships, family or communities that understand, hold and direct us into that which we "ought to be". Only now we understand how the "waiting around" of Hegel has nothing to do with the "abyss" of Nietzsche or that of the ancient Greeks. We rewrite the quote of Nietzsche:

> *"Verily, I had to fly to the highest spheres that I might find the fount of pleasure again. Oh, I found it, my brothers! Here, in the highest spheres, the fount of pleasure wells up for me. – Nietzsche."*

We are now in a position to claim that as long as there is no possibility of falling into the dreaded "abyss", that is, into the condition of the disoriented or fallen that the mind fears, genuine human thinking cannot and will not be. For, if anything, humans are το δεινότατον in that humans have the capacity to experience and exert δεινόν twice. That is, humans might "dare" to look at the abyss and the abyss might look back at them. We quote Nietzsche again:

> *"Beware that, when fighting monsters, you yourself do not become a monster... for when you gaze long into the abyss. The abyss gazes also into you. – Nietzsche."*

Avoiding the condition of the fallen as a possibility is avoiding to be human in the gazing, or otherwise in the possibility, to face and exert δεινόν. The "waiting around" of Hegel, in the sense of a true disorientation of the mind, is constitutive of humans in as far as it is a possibility that is always present to humans but has nothing to do with δεινόν. The "logics" that emerge as we are already oriented toward thinking, including those of Hegel or any other, are only an emergent phenomenon of the mind in as far as such "logics" are always facing the possibility to collapse. Through understanding the logic of Hegel and others, and precisely when we understand them best, our mind is protected and working at its best. In the whole of the logic of Hegel the mind is therefore very "far" from "collapsing" even if we face "nothingness" regarding thoughts that come to us even through contradictions. We must now clarify what we mean by humans being double δεινόν, that is το δεινότατον. What δεινόν is, is expressed in the next lines by Heidegger's reading of Heraclitus and Sophocles:

> *"On the one hand, δεινόν names the terrible, but it does not apply to petty terrors and does not have the degenerate, childish, and useless meaning that we give the word today when we call something "terribly cute." The δεινόν is the terrible in the sense of the overwhelming sway, which induces panicked fear, true anxiety, as well as collected, inwardly*

> *reverberating, reticent awe. The violent, the overwhelming is the essential character of the sway itself. – Heidegger."*

> *"On the other hand, δεινόν means the violent in the sense of one who needs to use violence—and does not just have violence at his disposal but is violence-doing, insofar as using violence is the basic trait not just of his doing but of his Dasein ("condition of humans"). – Heidegger."*

Heidegger also wrote:

> *"Humans are δεινόν twice, in a way that is unique to humans, that is, το δεινότατον. Humans exert violence and are the most violent: violence-doing in the midst of the overwhelming violence. – Heidegger."*

We leave any further reading of Heidegger to the reader but suffice it to say that δεινόν, in the above lines, refers to what humans are. Humans are always facing the possibility to "lose their minds" as much as they have the possibility to "have a mind". While we have a mind, we might also "face the abyss". We are in this way always confronted by the possibility of a sway. That humans are το δεινότατον was stated by Sophocles in what Heidegger interpreted above:

> *"Manifold is the uncanny, yet nothing uncannier than man bestirs itself, rising up beyond him. - Sophocles."*

If in the above sentence "uncanny" is to be understood as δεινόν and "nothing uncannier" as το δεινότατον we can proceed to describe what the sentence says. Humans are δεινόν in that 1) the gazing at the abyss and at the ungrounded grounds that uproot is always a possibility to the human and 2) in that one might always come back from the abyss with an ungrounded ground that uproots. As humans fear facing the "abyss" they face δεινόν and they dwell in its vicinity. Humans further place the abyss in front of others with their "violent" imposition of their "saying". In this way they are δεινόν themselves, i.e. humans are δεινόν twice.

## Pointing at what "is" the object of the mind

In the next lines and chapters, we describe the structure of the mind and the phenomenological workings of the mind as:

1) the "gazing or looking" at the "abyss" and the uprooting of the ungrounded grounds,

2) the coming back from that gaze with the ungrounded ground that serves as our camping site. That is, as the site that holds us as we hold onto it and as we orient and direct ourselves toward a path,

3) the sway that might otherwise disorient and redirect us or otherwise totters or shakes our stance, and,

4) the confronting ourselves and others with our placing uprooting grounds as we say, ignore or appear as indifferent.

We return to self-help books and other similar fields and their sayings. First, in as far as these neglect humans in their uniqueness as το δεινότατον, such sayings cannot refer to the authentic and unique condition of humans. That is, they miss the condition of humans in as far as being human even if they "act" or "advice" the human to act or be in any possible way that humans "act" and "are". Copying the acts of humans, either by exploiting algorithms, deep learning, the exploitation of big data or other, will miss the condition of το δεινότατον when such methods are "directed" from the fields that already conform toward a "toward". Let these be neurology, psychology or other. For the same reason they cannot fundamentally claim anything about the fallen, as the abyss and the falling remain alien to them – the motivational sentences then appear to the abyss and to το δεινότατον "like dogs that bark at what they don't know - Heraclitus". We state this formally now: whether the falling is to be avoided is not and cannot be fundamentally answered in a direction and orientation that is already given before any call to "face" the "abyss" even took place. That is, before one even dares to "lean toward" that which calls to be thought about, the questioning of falling appears as alien and concealed. The condition of fallen and the "abyss" emerge as "absent" in these sayings in that a direction is always and already delivered. Heraclitus claims that hearing while not understanding puts us in the condition of absent present. This was said before, but we rewrite it for emphasis:

> *"Those who hear without the power to understand are like deaf people; Present, they are absent. – Heraclitus."*

The sentences and message in motivational or self-help books, do not ignore the "abyss" in that they do not advice to fall, ignore the falling or neglect the question by rejecting it. The sentences and sayings "ignore" the abyss in that for them the "abyss" is ignored even in the act of ignoring it. That is, in that they do not "originate" or consider the "abyss" as a possibility, they can't even claim to be indifferent to it. If any, any mention of the abyss and ungrounded uprooting appears as an "inconvenience" to be pushed aside. On the other hand, and while the "abyss" is alien to them, motivational sentences take their direction in as far as the "abyss" and το δεινότατον are what is at stake in these sentences. These are at stake in that such phenomena always emerge as a "menace" to the directionality of the mind. That is, a motivational sentence or a call to "straighten up" our lives are threatened to shake and collapse by the sight of the abyss. A genuine call however, will consider the abyss, even if ignoring it, and emerge from the condition of δεινόν twice so to appear genuinely and authentically in the condition that is unique to humans. That is, as if uprooting. Motivational and self-help books in general otherwise appear as "logical" in their direction and as "real" as they point toward that "which directed them through their call". Their call is many times the avoiding of falling and loss of direction of the mind, at all cost, even as a possibility. In that way, as they direct, these sentences are already on their way to their path. They are "instruments" with a target. For the same reason, their methods, excelling or correctness in fulfilling targets cannot be claimed to "act" as a grounding ground not as authentic uprooting as they are "repeated" or "taken". But rather, their directionality is taken directly from a condition of uprooting that ignores the uprooting as a possibility. The uprooting appears "blurred" and as if "buried" by words. Taking the direction of the words however is what we call "understanding" as we listen to the "sayings" and "lean toward" them to orient us. If we are to understand, we are to listen to the sayings and conform. If we conform with what is said, we must be conscious as we "listen" to what is said and "lean toward" it. How does being absent present involve such obviously well intended sentences if we understand them and conform with them? In that by being already directed we cannot hear any other. As we are already directed, we appear as the absent present, that is, we appear unconscious. The "positive" direction of self-help books and motivational quotes is otherwise "to be taken" to an "end". Both their direction and their end are grounded in their consistency as a saying to an end. That these are "positively" formulated tools is not to be ignored, in the same way that we are not to ignore the success of science and technology. Their sayings however are not our theme, our theme is the phenomena of such "sayings" that occur as "sayings" as we discussed above.

We now direct our attention back to Hegel's paragraph above. We recall that the "abyss" of Hegel is always to be seen as "radically different" from that of Nietzsche and the ancient Greeks. This radical difference can only refer already to the gap in the metaphysics that separates our modern thinking from the Greeks. In his main book "Being and time" Heidegger wrote:

> *"And when Hegel at last defines 'Being' as the 'indeterminate immediate' and makes this definition basic for all the further categorial explications of his 'logic', he keeps looking in the same direction as ancient ontology ... 'Being' ... cannot mean ... clearest... It is rather the darkest (concept) of all. – Heidegger."*

So, what for Hegel was clearest and most indeterminate, for the ancient Greek metaphysics was determinate, yet the darkest of all. This is to clarify the distance in our metaphysics as modern humans as compared to ancient Greeks. We only need to think of humans as το δεινότατον in order to appreciate that ancient pre-Socratic sayings about what humans "are" remain alien to us as modern people, at least academically, or formally.

Let us read what modern Wikipedia has to say about what humans are in its entry on humans:

> *"Humans (taxonomically, Homo sapiens) are the only extant members of the subtribe Hominina. They (humans) are characterized by erect posture and bipedal locomotion; high manual dexterity and heavy tool use compared to other animals; open-ended and complex language use compared to other animal communications; and a general trend toward larger, more complex brains and societies. – Wikipedia"*

The above definition reminds us of Hegel's dialectics in terms of formalism and it is clearly very distant to the δεινόν of the Greeks. To the ancient Greeks humans are το δεινότατον, not a "member of Hominina characterized mostly by its posture, the use of complex language and their larger brains". That we "clearly" understand the entry of Wikipedia but feel very distant to the saying that humans are το δεινότατον speaks for itself in the distantiality of our metaphysics with respect to that of the ancient Greeks. On the other hand, this distance is only apparent. As far as academic formality goes, we appreciate the entry of Wikipedia. On the other hand, in our everyday lives we might say, even if sometimes: "Humans are crazy.", "Humans are the cruellest of all." or "You never know with people". That we "know", even if vaguely, what the Greeks meant by το δεινότατον when appealing to our everyday lives but cannot understand it "formally", speaks of a distance between what humans "are" and the "toward" of "toward where" that humans are "led to" overall as a species. If any, the "toward" must come from academic and formal "saying" that appears otherwise alien to το δεινότατον. That the question of what "is" was not to be turned into an academic business was noted by Heraclitus:

> *"Pythagoras inquired farther than all men, and, deciding what he liked among his thoughts, claimed a wisdom of his own. Much learning is mere fraud. – Heraclitus."*

We now return to the term waiting around as it is still relevant in that "waiting around" seems to be essential to consciousness in Hegel's view, even if as a "succession in the process or progress toward a goal". In as far as Hegel's is somehow a "formal" modern "logic", even if metaphysical, we might still use it to "think". Other forms of logic, such as informal logic or natural language could be considered, but we are not to follow such path here. In any case, Hegel claims that we "must", "await the process", "progress", or "wait around" before we point at the new object of thought. That new object of thought will somehow become our object of thought and dictate the orientation of our minds. In Hegel's terminology we could say we need to wait for "the movement of the spirit". This movement of the spirit is therefore essential before we can point. According to Hegel our new "object of thought" and "orientation of the mind" springs up from "nothingness". In any case, this "waiting around" must relate to waiting in as far as waiting relates to searching as we look at the "abyss of the unthought", that is, as we search as if without direction towards "an emerging thought". After all, the "waiting around", according to Hegel, comes only after everything collapses in as far as it comes after "nothingness or emptiness" has met us in the abyss of "contradiction". Hegel wrote:

> *"The skepticism that ends up with the bare abstraction of nothingness or emptiness cannot get any further from there, but must wait to see whether something new comes along and what it is, in order to throw it too into the same empty abyss – Hegel."*

With these thoughts we can already direct our minds toward what will come in the next chapter:

> *"The object of thought and the orientation of the mind, acts as a camping site that raises up against all other in as far as the holding with the mind points firmly but might otherwise fall."*

We recall that falling goes by rank. Waiting around is so weak of a term that it does not do justice to the term "abyss" and δεινόν as expressed in the previous section when discussing Heraclitus, Sophocles and Heidegger. This might be why Heidegger also claimed that Hegel looks at the past history of ontology in order to conclude, but never at the essence of the pre-Socratic thinking, nor to the future of thinking, and dismissed the determinacy of being. Being remained "indeterminate" for Hegel in that "reality" and what "is" remains indeterminate the more general what "is" is. This concept reminds us of the tendency of modernly saying that what "is" is a point of view or opinion and that all opinions are valid regarding what "is". We modernly still tend to believe however that there "is" a reality but also points of view. We might still give opinions and points of view lower rank relative to the rank that we give that which "is". Here, we particularly focus and speak of that which "is" when our everyday lives are at stake. At this point, it is worth clarifying that we are not claiming that we do not "think" when we do academic work, "logics" of our everyday life or other. Whether we fall to the "waiting around" of the "abyss" of Hegel or the "dreadful" but otherwise "blissful" "abyss" of Nietzsche is a falling of the mind as it "seeks". It is all the same a possibility for a thought to come to the front even if such coming belongs to a different rank. The "thinking" of the sciences however, or what we might call "modern" thinking in our everyday lives, is not what we will discuss here. Such thinking is being researched and studied well by the fields that concern it. The relationship between such thinking and the human mind has also been already discussed in a previous chapter. Here, we are discussing the coming of the "is" as what "is" comes to our minds in our everyday lives. We might say: "That is what I meant.", "That is very good." or "That is bad.". In such occasions where our lives are "at stake" there is an "is" and opinions appear as "words" to deceive. There is then a sway between "just opinions" being what is, and the "is" of being what "truly is". In that we constantly reaffirm ranking as we live we might understand the quote of Heidegger above that we repeat here:

> *"They continually deal with beings everywhere. Yet Being remains concealed to them. If Being is to open itself up, it itself must have rank and maintain it. – Heidegger."*

The possibility of seeing what "is" as relative or opinion, specially where our lives are not at stake, emerges as phenomena of the mind in our everyday lives. The "waiting around" of Hegel is in this way only related to the "abyss" and δεινόν in that there is only a partial "losing track" or "losing site of all" when such losing track remains alien to the mind. It then becomes a "saying" that is "said". Waiting around appears as an alien "waiting" that concerns us only as "waiting" for something to emerge. The waiting remains alien to a "losing track" or a "staying on track" of our living our lives. The questioning of Hegel is in this way alien to the falling of the mind. Such saying of the "sayings" that are "just said" however still emerges as phenomena of the mind. We deal with such "dealing" with things that are alien to us but make us "think" and "wait for thought", even if only as we "think" about sayings. In the "waiting around" of Hegel there is still a "toward", a "need" and an "is" in as far as there is the "living our lives". That is, there is "everyday" phenomena as a "task at hand". On the other hand, the mind genuinely "sees" or glances at the "abyss" that is expressed as δεινόν in Sophocles' tragedy when the mind itself has lost itself. In such "losing track" what "is" and what "is not" might not even be articulated. Uprooting is not possible from a task at hand that happens to be a task at hand. A "task at hand" does not even present itself when we "truly fall". Only as one orients oneself back, one can "uproot", as if stepping on an ungrounded ground that "orients" us. As one uproots up and "sees" one can "say" what "is". One has conviction, believes and is persuaded to "say". The ground is ungrounded in that it uproots but the ground still emerges and allows us to "say". In this way, in as far as one "sees" and "thinks", things are. According to Parmenides, that what "is" came from what it "is not" cannot be. Rather, using the terminology of Heidegger, what is concealed is to be revealed. So, the "nothingness" of Hegel must still be something to the mind as it "is". Parmenides wrote:

> *"It needs must be that what can be spoken and thought is;*
> *For it is possible for it to be, and it is not possible for what is*
> *nothing to be. This is what I bid thee ponder. – Parmenides."*

What "is" does not emerge from what "is not" as if what "is not" is hiding and waiting to be discovered and become what "is". That things are "hiding" is not what we mean when we say something remains concealed and then it is unconcealed when it "is". What remains concealed still "is" in its possibility to "uproot". What is, "is", always was and will always be. Provided it uproots it always had the possibility to "uproot". What is "is" as the mind "sees" and as what "is" "uproots". What "is" is fully as the mind brings it to the front. That truth comes with resoluteness, conviction and passes the test of being was said by Parmenides in his fragment:

> *"First of the Truth's unwavering heart that is fraught with conviction, Then of notions of mortals, where no true conviction abideth. – Parmenides".*

We have made several references to words that are "just said", the thinking academically or intellectually and other types of thinking as opposed to the "thinking" what "is". That we have emphasized these points so much relates to the familiarity of knowing that sometimes when we say, things "truly" are in that we "know" they "are". That such "knowing" is so "ambiguous" and "familiar" is then "hiding" a very subtle phenomenon of the mind. If we could measure from the "subtlety" of what comes to us as "familiar", and the difficulty to articulate what "is", the "depth" of the "abyss", we could say that the "abyss" here is without a bottom. The question is simple, we repeat it many times as we live our lives, yet, we say it is without bottom. As we deal with it continuously we give our backs to it. We repeat the sentence of Heraclitus:

> *"For they turn their backs on that with which they traffic the most, λόγος, and what they run into every day appears alien to them. – Heraclitus."*

Only through the asking the question one can understand the bottomless of asking. If we are to understand whether an AI or any from of artificial being is to be considered human, or behave as a human, one could measure from the distance of this question alone. The question is simple. What "is"?

If we are to know who we are as opposed to what machines are, this question becomes crucial. That the ancient Greeks dealt with this question but already where getting familiar with it to the point of obviating it was already noted by Heraclitus. Heraclitus noted the "turning" academic of the question that involves "wisdom", that is, the question regarding what "is". Heraclitus said:

> "Pythagoras inquired farther than all men, and, deciding what he liked among his thoughts, claimed a wisdom of his own. Much learning is mere fraud. – Heraclitus."

For clarity we provide another translation:

> "Pythagoras practiced research most of all men, and making extracts from these treatises he compiled a wisdom of his own, an accumulation of learning, a harmful craft. – Heraclitus."

If much learning is mere fraud, much learning cannot refer to the targeted knowledge of doing as a craft. Let alone of understanding academics, building or other. The learning of the sciences, academics, engineering or other, is "excluded" from the "wisdom" that Heraclitus referred to as learning here. It is excluded because such learning is legitimately passed on from one to another as crafting. The learning can only relate to a question that no matter how much we enquire, it always presents itself as bottomless. This can only be the question of what "is". That is, the crucial question for Heraclitus and Parmenides.

The era of predictive AI focuses on that which can be predicted by singling out what truly is and why it is logical that what is "is". It otherwise provides arguments that do not and cannot point as they never face the "abyss" and can never be "oriented" nor lack "orientation". If standard predictive AI doubts or "loses track" in a way that simulates human confusion, it does so in the sense of Hegel's "waiting around" at most. What "is" on the other hand, cannot be for these entities because "uprooting" is not even contemplated. Hegel's philosophy is, because of the way it speaks about what is, extremely subtle in how the emergent phenomena of the mind might be missed in its sayings. For example "waiting around", "progress of the mind", "succession in the process" and other are so passive and "unnatural", as they lack strength as one tries to interpret δεινόν from these. Neglecting and forgetting the question regarding what being is, as we are already pointing toward the object of thought that is delivered at hand, is the beginning of this curious current view of the terms "truth", "logics" and "reality" as the whole of what is. We might even reduce "thinking" to the "thinking" directed to what we already take as what "is". The question in this way is passed over and neglected. The modern target is an answer, never a question. Modern sayings might go "I can give you all the answers that you need" or "We have the answer to your question". Considering questioning itself and for itself is, in principle, not even considered. The questioning of what we "are", what we "need" and what our "toward" is, is, in this way neglected, even if, as Heraclitus says, we deal with it continuously. In our everyday lives we continuously speak of the "what" of what "is". Still, even asking the question "what is?" seems ridiculous in the sense that it seems to be asking nothing. More striking, even though neglecting these questions, we still "think". We miss the call and do not even "see" other but we "progress" and "advance" toward a "toward" even if such "toward" in ambiguously articulated. We appear as unconscious to other in as far as we are already oriented. Is it not dreadful, i.e. δεινόν, that someone can be directed by happiness or peace of mind without asking, or even acknowledging as a possibility, the question of what is? The possibility to live without asking emerges as δεινόν and as fundamental structure of the mind. That we now call this condition "superficial life" does not do justice to the question in that avoiding asking the question by placing the word "superficial" in a sentence instead is still ignoring the question itself. A genuine asking of the question appears as "unavoidable" as we can't manage to attend its call. We have no time as we "take the task at hand" and "move on". Is this not evidence enough even though we "say" that we can potentially think we are still not thinking? Is not the avoiding the question, and even fearing the asking of the question, evidence enough that we have not learnt to think? Maybe now we are ready to listen to the sentence of Heidegger rather than taking it as a "saying". We rewrite the saying of Heidegger:

> *"Everything thought-provoking gives us to think ... as far as it already is intrinsically what must be thought*

*about… Most thought-provoking is that we are still not thinking – Heidegger."*

Hegel was, in this sense, not "looking", "listening" nor "leaning toward" a call, since he was already "oriented". What is, cannot be what it is not for the mind. One is missing the phenomena of the mind if one ignores the emergent phenomena in the workings of the mind, that is, the "striking", the "fearful", the "abyss" and, in summary, the condition of δεινόν and its possibility in terms of determinacy in its "saying" and "seeing". We might get some understanding of Hegel's directiveness if we consider his travelling through the Alps. In a biography Althaus wrote[37]:

> *"Hegel's descriptions of the journey nowhere reveal any sense of awe or astonishment in the face of the overpowering might of the mountains around him. … "I doubt whether the most devout of theologians would dare to ascribe the virtue of utility for the human to nature herself in these mountain regions…""*

Hegel already turned the whole of what "is" into a "craftsmanship" and was therefore alien to the ancient question of what "is". Hegel was, in this sense, already modern. Only by considering such alienation from the phenomena of the mind, and considering a description of "logical" sayings, as seen in modern times, as what "is", one can understand that "waiting around" can never be translated into the facing the abyss in the sense of Nietzsche, Parmenides, Heraclitus or Sophocles. We might be asked to understand a set of sentences because of the inherent logics in them, that is, because of the inherent "reality" in the sentences that point, truly, to what truly is. Such logics can be "understood" by the mind through its workings, but it is constitutive of the phenomena of the mind only in that the mind can "perform". Without orienting our mind toward the call for thinking however, how can a neighborhood of thought stand as the ground or camping site for any "truth", "logics" or "reality"? How can any "logics" deploy? Without reorienting our minds toward the orientation or direction of what presents itself as what is, that is, the immediacy of thought presenting itself as what is, how could "what is" oppose itself and confront itself to become what is not? Let us quote Hegel again:

> *"The "opposing sides" are different definitions of consciousness and of the object that consciousness is aware of or claims to know - Hegel."*

The opposing sides of Hegel, as far as το δεινότατον, are a formality and have therefore nothing to do with the uprooting or the facing of "losing our mind". Let us quote Heraclitus and Hegel in what they say:

> *"Being is not more than Non-being – Heraclitus"*

> *"Being and non-being are the same – Hegel."*

The being and non-being of Heraclitus maintain rank in that what is "is" and uproots from the "abyss" as a violent placing. The origin is always the same, the uprooting that lives near the menace that can unground it all. The mind is always at stake by facing the "monster" that can, at any time, come to us as we "lose our mind". The being that is the same as non-being for Hegel, is a formality that emerges from a "waiting around" even if the mind loses site of any thought. That both sentences speak of phenomena of the mind does not mean that one is superior to the other. On the other hand, the unique condition of humans cannot be reduced to a craftsmanship as long as the "directing" of what "is" might at any time come as a "violent placing" or simply fall.

As the mind and the objects of thought come to the mind to hold us as if gathering onto a camping site that directs us, thoughts and orientations genuinely come only as a daring. Thoughts call us from the empty abyss of nothingness where the unthought dwells concealed. As we fall into the abyss, the abyss might look back and call us. Provided we are ready to listen, we might hear the call and uproot strongly as we say. Any other thought can only be, in comparison, something that was already given and therefore not complete as far as the uniqueness in humans. The situation of the fallen is, always and necessarily, disorienting, not because of thoughts, the objects of thought or because we are human, but because of its essence.

That the world provides objects of thought, directions and answers, but always avoids the falling into the abyss, is as concerning as intriguing. Through science, arts and sports the mind will always find an object of thought provided and toward which the orientation of the mind is always given, beforehand and neglecting above all, the possibility to fall. These statements might sound at least shocking: "even art will not let us think and be". That even art can become a tool to dehumanize humans might sound shocking only if we have already been thus directed and oriented. In the condition of the fallen we are told to not stay. We are told to ignore it as a possibility. In this way, by being always directed and oriented, the human cannot "hear" nor "say", and cannot, by necessity, reorient its mind to the call for genuine thinking. The condition of the fallen is so feared that it is, in any case, not even considered as a call. The condition of the human is always directed to a direction, any direction will do, provided it keeps us away from the abyss of the fallen. Thus, while conscious of a direction and an orientation that can only be one, arguments, logics and truth can always follow but not dare. Without daring, any call cannot be heard, and humans cannot hear. The human can only conform. Humans will appear conscious to one only, but to none other. To the hearing of the call they will appear as if unconscious and the abyss of the unthought will remain concealed.

# Saying, Listening and Seeing

## The mind, what "is" and the unfolding of history

In following our question for why truth and logics have become the whole of what is, we turn to the word λόγος and its interpretation in ancient Greek by the readings of Heraclitus, Parmenides, Sophocles, Heidegger and others. From these writings we borrow as the foundation of awareness the meaning of λόγος as what comes together, that is, what has immediacy, comes together and gathers. Through λόγος what can be understood is understood by what is already conforming. We provide now some quotes regarding λόγος:

> *"Saying and hearing are authentic and proper only when they are intrinsically directed - and oriented - in advance toward λόγος. – Heidegger."*

> *"But those who do not grasp λόγος are able neither to hear nor to say – Heraclitus."*

The interpretation of λόγος and what it means to direct toward λόγος will be described in the next pages. Suffice it to say that we will describe the condition of being human and a perpetual sway between falling, orientation and reorientation toward what holds us as "who we are". We now give three preliminary points (by Heidegger[38]) that will further assist us in our discussion:

*1. The determination of the human essence is never an answer, but is essentially a question.*

This is always the question of what "is".

*2. The asking of this question is historical in the originary sense that this questioning first creates history.*

*3. This is the case because the question of what humanity is can be asked only in questioning about Being.*

That the human essence is not an answer but involves always a question was already mentioned in the previous chapter, even if implicitly. As humans are δεινόν twice, the uniqueness of humans relates to the possibility to confront and face the "abyss" of nothingness, from where everything uproots, or otherwise place with violence by invoking such "uprooting". Even when the "abyss" emerges only ambiguously and rarely, its presence is always familiar both as a "menace" and as a source of directions in the "need" and "seeking" of the mind to be directed. Both the facing the "abyss" and the uprooting from the "abyss" present humans as an uninterpreted "sign" or "enigma". Questioning such "enigma" creates history in that such questioning is always related to the attempt to look at the essence of humans in the face or simply obviating it. That is, even in the "obviating" of the question, the "enigma" is present as the menace of a "tottering", "shaking" or absolute "collapse" but also as a foundation, even if groundless. What comes from such questioning exposes to humans what it "is" to be human even in the possibility to "totter" and "collapse" but also to "uproot" by placing "grounds". The "is" that results from the question always comes to direct us, even if the "is" is "ambiguously" or "unclearly" presented and even if the question resulting with the "is" obviates the question itself. In this way, the direction of the "is" creates history in all cases as the "is" is always directed even if ambiguously and even if lacking a grounding ground. That is, the questioning of "Being" determines the essence of humans in that it "directs" and "orients" us toward that "which we are" in a way that the question clears a path ahead. A path that essentially determines the history of what we are as the "task at hand" is always on its way to its path directionally. The "task at hand" thus directs us as it emerges as "the truly real" object of the mind and as its direction as the historical direction that "guides" us. Humans "see" what guides them even if not clearly and even if ambiguously. As we are "guided" we create "history" in the direction of what "guides" us. This is so even in the shaking of what guides us. We are now at a point where a question might come to mind: how is this "intriguing" relationship between the questions for the "is" and the "needs" of "humans" and the phenomena of the mind that has emerged so far to be understood? The three sentences above and the respective interpretation given so far provide an answer.

## Saying, listening and seeing

We start by quoting[39] several authors regarding language and a running up against language[40]:

> *"All that we can say can only, a priori, be nonsense. Nevertheless we run up against the boundaries of language – Wittgenstein."*

> *"Kierkegaard too saw that there is this running up against something and he referred to it in a fairly similar way (as running up against a paradox). This running up against the limits of language is ethics – Wittgenstein on Kierkegaard."*

> *"What, you scoundrel, you would speak no nonsense? Go ahead and speak nonsense – it doesn't matter! – Holy Augustine."*

> *"The property of 'goodness' cannot be defined. It can only be shown and grasped. Any attempt to define it will simply shift the problem. It is a priori certain: whatever one may give as a definition of the Good – it is always only a misunderstanding to suppose that the expression corresponds to what one actually means - G.E. Moore."*

> *"What is said in λόγος as what comes together, implies what can be understood is understood by what is already conforming – Heidegger."*

> *"There is nothing that we are more used to than consciousness but at the same time there is nothing that we understand the least - John Searle"*

*Sergio Santos, Matteo Chiesa and Maritsa Kissamitaki.*

> *"Rising high over the site, losing the site is he for whom what is not, is, always, for the sake of daring – Sophocles."*

We many times appeal to the consciousness of others with sentences like "Don't you see?", "Can't you see?", "Don't you see the truth that is in front of you?", "I can't believe you don't see reality!" or "I wish you understood what I mean because it's obvious and real!". We find ourselves in a situation of despair when a conscious being, i.e. another human, does not understand. Not being understood by a human seems illogical and unreasonable since humans are the rational beings that can think and understand. Yet, sometimes we can't even understand ourselves and request ourselves attention and understanding. That is, sometimes we say we need to listen and pay attention to our "selves". All these sentences, calls and expressions are so common in everyday language that it seems many times we are not conscious and cannot reason. Then what does it mean that we can reason and understand?

Before we answer the question regarding understanding we can focus on another question: what does it mean to call? What does it mean to request for consciousness to manifest by attending to what calls? What is it that is calling us? To explore what the requests are calling for, we might start by thinking about the requests in the questions that request our attention. These are calls to attract the attention of humans as if requesting that thought is redirected toward a direction or path. These questions and expressions are requests to a human's consciousness to be directed and pointed toward what calls and appears in a given situation as essential. These calls might come from others, from our "self", our "true deep self", our "being ourselve with others" or anything else, in any form and anywhere. If we pay attention to these requests, we can almost feel a rerouting that redirects a flow of thought. We feel this rerouting as we start to pay attention to what calls our attention or as we see, in someone else, the rerouting of their attention to what we, or they, consider to be essential. Rerouting or redirecting happens in a way that can remind us of a pointer that redirects as an arrow that can then flow. We can also describe this request as a request for the attention of the one that listens to a call. In any case, what is at stake is attention and a readiness to redirect and listen. [41]

It is now a target to create artificial debating machines that debate in the form of arguments that provide evidence supporting the validity of what is said and is to be communicated. Debating by providing arguments in favor or against a cause however does not suffice to humans and cannot suffice. To understand, a human's mind is first requested to point in the direction of what is essential and calls to be pointed at. Humans must lean and incline to what is said. Anything said in the form of logical arguments before this happens "might not be heard". Instead, attention needs to be redirected and pointed into the requested direction. Only then, one listens. Without pointing and directing, to humans, evidence and arguments cannot refer to anything and logics and arguments cannot flow. A human might otherwise choose to not "hear".

If consciousness was about "listening" to that which is logical, any "listening machine" with a microphone could listen and record. But a machine cannot "listen" even if it listens through a microphone to record. If consciousness could be addressed by learning data in terms of storage, we could argue that the storing of knowledge would have already acted as a tool to construct a conscious entity. What a conscious entity is however is still to be questioned. That is, even if we simulated consciousness in the sense that it could pass a test for "consciousness", what that would mean would remain to be questioned. Even the question to be asked however remains enigmatic. That we do not even know how to pose the question of what consciousness is, is in this sense intriguing and striking. In short, knowing and storing data, by itself, does not provide a conscious person the means to retain, maintain or hold consciousness. Data might build a neighborhood for thought but does not include the arrow of thought or the possibility for a thought and a direction to totter or otherwise stand firm to "see". A device that stores data does not and cannot "look" or "see" even if it has eyes and can distinguish between things. Consciousness needs to point. When we feel that we lack consciousness, even as humans, we have no "look", we cannot "see", we have lost our capacity to point with our minds. When we cannot pay attention to what calls for attention by manifesting itself as essential we claim that we are not conscious. It is in these cases that our consciousness is requested to become conscious with the above questions. In that way, we appeal to our consciousness to point.

Even if we understood that we point and attend to things by pointing at them with our minds, there is still the question of what it is that we must point at. Even if we point at something, where is the pointing leading us? The "toward where" that that pointer takes us is in this way at stake. While humans pay attention and continuously point at things, our beginning and our end remains enigmatic. On the other hand, we might say our minds are always busy with matters. It is then not only that we point at things with our minds that makes us the being that can reason. Rather, it is our capacity to decide to either hold our pointing or redirect it to other matters that call us that makes others claim that we are conscious, including our "selves". This is what we meant before with our capacity to "hold consciousness in" or otherwise "open it up".

The question remains on what it is that calls us. We say that what calls us gets our attention to redirect our minds to point toward it as it appears to us as essential. To point requires for there to be a path or track. The pointing refers us to the orienting of ourselves onto a track that calls us as essential. So, what is it that is essential? That which calls us in a way that it requests to be pointed at and explored with the conscious mind. Redirecting our mind to point toward what calls us requires a leap, it requires that we dare and rank this over that. Redirecting requires neglecting above all, that is, a falling or dropping of our direction in benefit of "other". Only after we redirect our mind and hold it by pointing at it, logics can unfold and understanding manifests. This is the "opening up" of our consciousness to what calls us. We then say: "I see" or "now I understand". In that way, once we point at what called us, evidence and arguments become meaningful and might appear as logical and clear. When a person speaks logically with arguments, logics and evidence, the person stands firm. The person is held together. Consciousness is pointing in that what we point at is what holds us. Put as a question: how is what we point at our consciousness? In that it holds us as we confront and face all other. There are many sayings in English that remind us of consciousness as what holds us. For example, "losing oneself", "falling apart", "pulling ourselves together" and "bringing ourselves back to reality". All these sentences refer to a losing of balance or a losing of that which held us firm and together or a "gaining" ourselves back. In this way, expressions that act as requests to get our consciousness back ask for a way to get ourselves back on track. How do we bring ourselves back? We bring ourselves back by pointing at what holds us. Something that points at a path involves orientation. In that way, we point at what holds us by orienting our consciousness into that which holds us above all other. We are held in that we are rightly oriented toward a path and into a neighborhood of thoughts. Provided it holds us, any available data, arguments or logics will assist us into building a neighborhood as we point at what holds us. As we point at what holds us we leave everything else behind, as if concealed, to shed light onto the path ahead of us that opens itself to exploration. A path opens in front of us and becomes clear as all other paths close. As we point at what holds us, we stand firm, on a ground and neighborhood of thought that opens in what is otherwise ungrounded and concealed, i.e. the abyss of the unthought, the abyss that presents itself and ourselves as δεινόν. The abyss of unthought remains concealed as we point, in a way that the unthought is not, and cannot be, provided we are pointing toward what holds us. We clarify now with emphasis:

> *"What calls us for our attention opens as a single path as we redirect our mind and point at it. As we point at it, a path opens up as a site that gathers our thoughts."*

How does the path take us to a site? The path that we point at takes us to a site in that thoughts approach us and become what is near to us, that is, our neighborhood of thoughts. We might camp on this site and ground our thoughts up and above what holds us. The camping site becomes our site and its grounding becomes our grounding in that we lose all other sites as well as the ungrounded of the grounding of the site. The site's ground becomes our ground in as far as we point at what calls us and what calls us holds us. We are at a point where we can quote Nietzsche again:

> *"Verily, I had to fly to the highest spheres that I might find the fount of pleasure again. Oh, I found it, my brothers! Here, in the highest spheres, the fount of pleasure wells up for me. – Nietzsche."*

Our firm standing on our grounds is, on the other hand, as grounded as what grounded it, i.e. the call for attention that called our attention and revealed a path that now is but that was otherwise concealed. The path is grounded in that it "uproots" from our "saying" in the condition of δεινόν. We can finally go back to the beginning of the discussion on consciousness through the sentences that we first wrote. We wrote that through language we run up against the paradox. Put as a question: what do we run up against in language? We run up against the grounding of our camping site where we gather thoughts as we hold to what we point at and as what we already conform to our grounding as we "see". As we "see" we "dare" to be "who" we are and "see" what we "see". We turn to a part of the tragedy of Sophocles again:

> *"Rising high over the site, losing the site is he for whom what is not, is, always, for the sake of daring – Sophocles."*

Appealing to our human experience with examples can bring clarity to what has been said about a mind that orients us. Let us consider how mental collapse disorients us and how by genuinely listening to others the mind might first lose orientation but then redirect to genuinely listen to the call of others or to any other call. Once a call is heard, the mind takes direction and orientation, things become clear and we say "we see". A direction comes with "a task at hand". When someone loses their mind, we might say "he doesn't know where he is" or "she lost her mind" or "they lost track of time and space". When listening to someone's saying we might say "do you follow me?", "have I lost you?", "do you see my point?". When someone does not seem to know how to deal with an instrument we might say "he is lost" or "he doesn't know what he is doing with that instrument". When someone finds the way to operate an instrument they might say "I found it". Humans excel as they are "set" and on their way to their task. Humans excel as soon as they are "directed" and "oriented". Humans excel as soon as they "see" their path ahead in that this "seeing" gives us "legitimacy". As we "see" the way, we are set to the task of invoking what "is". This might as well be why humans excel at preparing and designing equipment. Equipment and technology are always oriented by a "task at hand" that provides a "toward" as soon as it "works as it should". In instruments there is a clear "seeing" the "what" and the "toward".

We might appeal to the coming back and to orient themselves back on track when people lose direction and orientation. In all these sayings we say that our minds' disposition and natural state is to be oriented or, at least, we have the capacity to direct and orient our minds if we wish to. When we are not oriented we appear as if unconscious. But unconscious of what and regarding what? When we are unconscious we miss a path that stands to orients us to that which calls us. We might claim that our natural position is that of being oriented as we already point at and toward a path. Yet we many times find ourselves reorienting ourselves looking for a path that will center us. We might find ourselves looking to point at a path as if disoriented. Is losing oneself through disorientation, that is, is the condition of the fallen, essential? In all listening to the "unknown" there is a sway between orientation and disorientation. Especially when listening, we get oriented as we listen, and we try and stay oriented and conscious as we point toward a call. But if we are still disoriented we are still at the mercy of a sway, collapse and fall. Language tells us that there is a track and a center and that our nature is to be on track and centered. We might say "center yourself" or "stay on track". We might question however the nature or even the existence of a real path or any path. Predictive AI, science, religion or other might say that there is a "real path". We might say there is a "real truth", a "strong argument" and a "logical set of logics". That there is a single track to follow in our listening to what calls us however is not a priori clear, let alone what the nature of this track is. Even less clear what "real", "truth" and "logics" means regarding the start of our journey toward a path or track. If we have followed this book - its path -, it becomes even less clear what "truth", "reality" and "logics" might mean before the direction and orientation of the mind takes place, that is, before the mind conforms to a path, a direction and an orientation. We started in the introduction with the intriguing question of what consciousness is and how it relates to understanding. There we said that understanding requires "already conforming". The sentence of Heidegger that we quoted goes:

> *"What is said in λόγος as what comes together, implies what can be understood is understood by what is already conforming – Heidegger."*

Only now the "already conforming" appears as an orientation to what "is" that is already in our mind as we set to "understand". There still remains the question of the "path". We can ask: if there was a path, how could we find it? That is, how do we get on track and how can we distinguish the track that will orient us? We point, direct and orient our mind toward the track or path that calls us. Humans however might hear many calls and might single one out as we dare to direct ourselves toward it by pointing and orienting our minds. When we are listening to a call and looking for a path we might say "I have lost track". When we think or listen we might say, "we heard the call and got on track". We might also say "we simply can't get the point" or that "we are missing something". In all these sayings there is an attempt to "lean toward" that which calls. This "leaning toward" what calls has emerged as the "positive" phenomenon of the mind that allows us to find a path. Once we are on track we explore and describe with the conscious mind as we stay firm on track. In this way, "we use logics". In this way the "logics", "truth" and "reality" that are erroneously taken as the origin and foundation, become and are. The day humans follow a single path of logics and never fall or lose their path, how will reorientation take place? The day humans do not fall to reorient and listen to the call of other than that toward what they are already directed and oriented, humans will become those that "cannot hear". We will be those that "are not conscious" no matter how much "truth" there is in what we "already see". We can turn again to the sentences of Heraclitus:

> *"They are like dogs: for dogs also bark at what they do not know – Heraclitus."*

> *"They are donkeys: donkeys like chaff better than gold. – Heraclitus."*

These sentences do not refer to people as those that do not know and do not prefer. The sentences of Heraclitus, in the same way, do not refer to humans in that humans "are good or evil" or "cannot think". The sentences refer to those that have "ears" but prefer to "not use them". To those that do not want to listen to the call, and thus, dismiss it by barking at it. The sentences refer to humans in as far as they are already and beforehand oriented toward other than the call. In this way, that other, i.e. what calls them, becomes something to bark at, or, in other words, something to throw logics and arguments onto even if these do not and cannot be as they do not refer to what "is". It would be otherwise grotesque that Heraclitus claimed that humans "cannot know" and "cannot understand". Heraclitus, in fact, respected humans in their "cleverness" and their "intelligence" even if "wisdom" was rare and some forms of it considered "harmful". For example, Heraclitus wrote:

> "It is wise to hear and listen, not to me, but to λόγος, and to confess that all things are one. – Heraclitus."

> "People that love wisdom must be acquainted with very many things indeed. – Heraclitus."

> "No one of all whose discourses I have heard has arrived at this result: the recognition that wisdom is apart from all other things. – Heraclitus."

Heraclitus is presumably speaking of those who, while not wise, know things in such fields as the technical, philosophical or political. Then, some people are intelligent and clever in many ambits, for example handcraftsmanship.

That the ancient Greeks believed in the cleverness of humans is also stated in the tragedy of Sophocles:

> "Clever indeed, for he masters skill's devices beyond expectation, now he falls prey to wickedness, yet again valor succeeds for him. Between the ordinance of the earth and the gods' sworn dispensation he fares. – Sophocles."

Yet Heraclitus claims we are like dogs and donkeys. How is a dog or a donkey to a human in that the dog or the donkey does not know and prefers one to the other? The dog might not be able to grasp the pointing nor the orientation of the mind of the human regarding the object of thought. Dogs and donkeys fail to direct and reorient their minds into the direction of the call for "seeing". Dogs "bark" and are not to "listen" to the call. Donkeys prefer "this" to "that" and are "not to listen" to other. Dogs and donkeys do not "lean toward" a call. In this way, only in as far as, and from the fallen, one can reorient and conform to a direction and an orientation, one can hear and say. Heraclitus says:

> *"But those who do not grasp λόγος are able neither to hear nor to say – Heraclitus."*

That humans cannot hear and say has to refer to a saying regarding that which they do not know. They do not know, presumably, because they do not grasp logos. If they did, they would know and be able to hear and say. Many lines above we said in a sentence what it means for humans to know in a way that will become clearer at this point. We repeat the sentence here for emphasis:

> *"Our mind can be directed and pointed toward all objects of thought, including the mind itself, and explore the neighborhood of that toward what it points at. In that way, things are known."*

If we do not point with our mind and explore what is to be known, by hearing the call or the invitation to "seeing" and thinking, things remain unknown, i.e. concealed. The remaining unknown here does not refer to the possibility that things, by themselves, contain truth, reality or strong logics. That is, we do not refer to things that are otherwise "true" in that they already are before and always. The knowing does not merely describe ignorance of what otherwise is. Knowing here genuinely refers to humans in that humans are "the ones that know". We repeat what we said as a statement for thinking: "arguments and logics" do not precede but come only, as we are already pointing, as what is to be known is already in front of us". Sophocles claimed humans "dare" to hear and say what they know thus rising beyond themselves. Saying in this way becomes barking and, like donkeys, as they did not manage to grasp, choose and prefer this over that or what is not to what is. Saying and hearing can then happen only as humans point with an orientation. Words and sounds are otherwise nothing to do with saying. They are only sounds or, as Heraclitus puts it, barks. Finally, we also refer to knowing in as far as knowing is not doing nor choosing. Once humans point and orient themselves toward a call, humans can know. We only subtly referred in the above writings however to what happens when humans know. As they know, humans might stand firm in what they know, or redirect and reorient toward what calls. Humans might also hear the call and firmly dismiss it. Humans confront, say, dare and sometimes listen. Our "attention", coming as the directionality of the mind toward that which "is in our mind" and "toward" that which "guides us", is in this way and many times "protected as precious". We might "give it", we might "protect it", we might "worry about it" or we might "seek" it. As we "say" to others, we invoke their attention. As we want others to "see" the what of what we mean, we invoke their "attention". Sometimes others "listen" to us and thus "attend" to what we say. Around us, everything manifests as if requesting our attention as we also request the attention of the world. The attention of others, and even all other, strikes us as we "listen" to it as much as when any other "listens" to us. As beings and things are, these always present the possibility to "speak for a matter" as long as we "lean toward" them as they speak. Through these actions humans are humans.

We now finish with another sentence from Heidegger and a call for thinking:

> *"The role of thinking is not that of an opponent. Thinking is thinking only when it pursues whatever speaks for a matter. – Heidegger."*

Heidegger said the above over 50 years ago. Today, artificial intelligence might use the word[42] "opponent" and claims the target of thinking is clarity and "rebuttal of the opponent". One does not have to look very far to find definitions of the exploration of intelligence and what it means to speak, think and listen: "debating consists on delivering with clarity and purpose an argument that will defeat the opponent." Regarding the exploration of the unthought and the listening to the call: "emotion, bias and ambiguity is to be avoided and preceded by evidence-based arguments". In this way, the sentences of predictive and assisting AI resonate in that they remind us of the methods of "self-help" books. Humans are guided into listening even if they did not hear a call. Humans cannot orient themselves as the direction and orientation is already at hand. The abyss of the unthought might in this way close and remain concealed. In this way the human becomes the one that cannot hear nor say as they already know. The human becomes the unconscious or another type of human. We might call it the human-object.

The human-object is not so termed because it "ambiguously" follows a path that is otherwise not "clear", that is, not "logical", "reasonable" or "real". It is not that it seems unconscious to others because it cannot "reason", "understand", deploy strong "logical arguments" or other. The human-object might in fact sound and appear purely conscious even to all around them, including its "selves", but still appear as if unconscious to a call. The unconscious of the human-object appears conscious in this way in a very concrete and specific way. In fact, as specific and delimiting as an orientation of the mind can be toward an object of thought of any type. One might further encounter ambiguity in that one "might not see a clear path" or might "act as if following inertia toward a path" but still hear the call by either paying attention or un-attending the call no matter how ambiguously or unclear the call might come to the front. Then, that an orientation and a direction prevail only "ambiguously", in that it has not been clarified as to the "where" or the "what" in terms of the object that "directs" our path, does not imply that a "direction" is not "leading" toward a "path" in a clear way. This merely means that a path is not "clearly" exposed unambiguously as a "path". Even if in such ambiguous path we cannot say, but we "simply feel", a path is still assumed. The feeling of ambiguity remains as vague and ambiguous unless a thought manifests and deploys as a clearing thought that was otherwise already around us as if hidden. As the clearing of the thought unveils a clear path, thought might come to the front with a strength that allows for "stronger logics" to deploy. On the other hand, staying in such ambiguous condition as to "follow" or "not follow" or not even "recognize" the ambiguity of a given path is not what we term here human-object. That is, surrounding oneself by such ambiguity is not what we term human-object, but quite the opposite. This is so because such staying in an otherwise condition of ambiguity does not imply that we cannot hear or attend to a call. We term human-object the staying and taking of a direction that came strongly and clearly within a margin that guides us and allows for logics to be deployed to an end, while veiling and silencing any possible call. In this way, the stronger and more robust a society becomes in its arguments, the stronger the tendency to the human-object might become. The "lack of ambiguity" or "emotions" cannot imply that we will be the ones that "hear", "say" or "see" but, on the contrary, we might appear as the ones that "do not hear, nor say nor see". That is, by already "knowing" and "seeing", we might simply appear as the "unconscious".

# Endnotes

1   We are not using the terminology of Karl Jaspers here in the sense the phenomena cannot be understood because it lacks coherence, but in the sense of "ungraspable". We also use quotation marks for the reader to think about the term, not just read it.

2   Parmenides, *The Fragments.* 2017: Amazon Digital Services LLC.

3   *Another translation might be: "for which Being and Non-Being are regarded as the same thing".*

4   Most references to Heraclitus are taken from the book: Heidegger, M., *Introduction to Metaphysics.* 2014: Yale University Press. Since most of our book makes reference to the philosophy of Martin Heidegger, his translations will be more suitable. On the other hand, the reader might refer to other translations for clarity and to contrast translations. For example, this fragment of Heraclitus is sometimes written as "Beginning and end are common to both ways."

5   Bohm, D., *Wholeness and the implicate order.* 1980: Routledge & Kegan Paul.

6   The quotes of Parmenides can be found in many English translations. While the reader can refer to any book in the literature such as Parmenides, *Fragments of Parmenides.* 2017: CreateSpace Independent Publishing Platform, or the first one we referenced, in our text we have employed many times the translation by Nolletti Albino that can be found online at http://www.parmenides-of-elea.net

7   Quotations on Heraclitus have been taken from Heraclitus, *The Fragments: of the Work of Heraclitus of Ephesus on Nature.* 1889: Amazon Digital Services LLC or Martin Heidegger's translation.

8   Bornedal, P., *The Surface and the Abyss: Nietzsche as Philosopher of Mind and Knowledge.* 2010: De Gruyter.

9   Nietzsche, F., *Delphi Complete Works of Friedrich Nietzsche.* 2015: Delphi Classics.

10  We recommend to the reader "Being and Time" by Heidegger. Heidegger, M., *Being and Time.* 2010: SUNY Press. The terms on the other hand are not employed in the remainder of our text.

11  https://phys.org/news/2012-04-quantum-function-reality.html#jCp

12  Colbeck, R. and R. Renner, *Is a System's Wave Function in One-to-One Correspondence with Its Elements of Reality?* Physical review letters, 2012. **108**(15): p. 150402.

13  For a discussion on the establishing of truth as a power structure in the institution we refer the reader to Foucault, M., *Madness and Civilization: A History of Insanity in the Age of Reason* 2013: Vintage.

14   The reader can refer to Heidegger's Being and time and particularly the chapter "Everyday Being-one's-Self and the "They"".

15   Our translation of Sophocles is taken direct from the book: "Heidegger, M., *Introduction to Metaphysics*. 2014: Yale University Press.

16   Here we refer to institution as any place where society has structure, i.e. family, work place, school or hospital.

17   Foucault, M., *The Order of Things: An Archaeology of the Human Sciences*. 1994: Vintage. We also recommend Foucault, M., *Madness and Civilization: A History of Insanity in the Age of Reason* 2013: Vintage.

18   https://en.wikipedia.org/wiki/John_Searle

19   https://www.independent.co.uk/news/uk/home-news/oxfam-crisis-latest-sexual-abuse-vulnerable-people-ngos-report-charity-commission-haiti-prostitutes-a8206431.html

20   https://www.theguardian.com/us-news/2018/aug/14/more-than-300-pennsylvania-priests-committed-sexual-abuse-over-decades

21   Descartes, R., *Discourse on the Method*. 2018: Createspace Independent Pub.

22   An example of this could be the very John Searle that is now accused of sexual assault and is, on the other hand, a main proponent of social reality. How he now argues with himself and others is to be seen.

23   Kleinridders, A., et al., *Insulin Action in Brain Regulates Systemic Metabolism and Brain Function*. Diabetes, 2014.

24   Frey, B.S., *What About a Happiness Pill?*, in *Economics of Happiness*. 2018, Springer International Publishing: Cham. p. 41-46.

25   Nasrallah, H.A., *eyond Dopamine: Brain Repair Tactics in Schizophrenia*. Current Psychiatry, 2015. **14**(6).

26   Swartz, J.R., A.R. Hariri, and D.E. Williamson, *An epigenetic mechanism links socioeconomic status to changes in depression-related brain function in high-risk adolescents*. Molecular Psychiatry, 2016. **22**: p. 209.

27   Meshi, D., D.I. Tamir, and H.R. Heekeren, *The Emerging Neuroscience of Social Media*. Trends in Cognitive Sciences, 2015. **19**(12): p. 771-782.

28   Gunter, B., *Is There a Link Between Playing Video Games and Social Violence?*, in *Does Playing Video Games Make Players More Violent?* 2016, Palgrave Macmillan UK: London. p. 93-114.

29   Bear, M.F., B.W. Connors, and M.A. Paradiso, *Neuroscience: Exploring the Brain*. 2015: Wolters Kluwer.

30   Lotto, B., *Deviate: The Science of Seeing Differently* 2017: Hachette Books.

31   Brugnoli, M.P., *Clinical Hypnosis in Pain Therapy and Palliative Care: A Handbook of Techniques for Improving the Patient's Physical and Psychological Well-being*. 2014: Charles C Thomas Pub Ltd.

32   http://www.un.org/en/universal-declaration-human-rights/

33   https://plato.stanford.edu/entries/hegel-dialectics/

34  https://en.wikipedia.org/wiki/Logic#Informal_reasoning_and_dialectic

35  Peterson, J.B., *12 Rules for Life: An Antidote to Chaos*. 2018: Random House Canada.

36  Pinker, S., *Enlightenment Now: The Case for Reason, Science, Humanism, and Progress*. 2018: Viking.

37  Horst Althaus, *Hegel: An Intellectual Biography*. 2000: Polity.

38  Heidegger, M., *Introduction to Metaphysics*. 2014: Yale University Press.

39  Ule, A., *Wittgenstein and Kierkegaard in and on paradox*. FILOZOFIA, 2014. **69**(5): p. 451-457.

40  Bell, J.A., A. Cutrofello, and P.M. Livingston, *Beyond the Analytic-Continental Divide: Pluralist Philosophy in the Twenty-First Century*. 2015: Routledge.

41  The word attention here also requires clarification. Attention is not only concerned with having senses or listening more clearly to all that is said and seen widely and openly. That one pays attention requires a narrowing in the sense of delimiting the scope of what is at our reach. In paying attention, we require that most of what is around becomes quiet and almost disappears so what call us for attention can appear more clearly in front of us as we attempt to point at it and enclose it. This description might strike us as odd if one considers what we now admire in people that we might claim to be open minded. Open minded however does not necessarily involve being open to all and stay open. Open minded might reflect the possibility of opening to then close and point at what was to be caught. If one stays open, one cannot attend to what calls. We might more readily understand attention as a narrowing of the scope that first points and then unfolds by considering current predictive AI and debaters.

42  https://www.research.ibm.com/artificial-intelligence/project-debater/

# About the Author

Dr Santos has spent more than ten years researching in the fields of bio/nanotechnology and data science.

Dr. Chiesa is a Professor materials sciences, alternative energies, fundamental nanoscale mechanics, dynamics and dissipation.

Maritsa Kissamitaki works in design, robot design, AI algorithm conceptualization, and fabrication and identifies as a generalist.

Printed in the United States
By Bookmasters